BEHIND THE STAR

Also by Gerald Butt

The Arab World – a Personal View (BBC Publications)

Gerald Butt

BEHIND THE STAR
Inside Israel today

CONSTABLE·LONDON

First published in Great Britain 1990
by Constable and Company Limited
3 The Lanchesters, 162 Fulham Palace Road
London W6 9ER
Copyright © Gerald Butt 1990
ISBN 0 09 469730 2

Set in Monophoto 11pt Sabon by
Servis Filmsetting Limited, Manchester
Printed in Great Britain by
St Edmundsbury Press Limited
Bury St Edmunds, Suffolk

A CIP catalogue record for this book
is available from the British Library

*For my mother and father
who spent so many years in the Middle East*

CONTENTS

ACKNOWLEDGEMENTS

My thanks go to all those who helped in the preparation of this book – not least those who agreed to be interviewed. Thanks also to those whose published thoughts I have quoted.

I am very grateful to my wife Lynne for help in collecting interviews in English, and to Ruthi Sudack for interviews and research in Hebrew.

Asher Wallfish kindly agreed to read the manuscript; and over the past three years he has been a patient and good-humoured guide to an outsider trying to understand the complexities of Israel.

G.B.
1990

FOREWORD

To commit words to paper about Israel is to lay down a challenge. Anyone considering doing so should understand this; in any event he or she will be made aware of it almost before the ink is dry. A challenge, because every word published, every syllable broadcast and every frame of film transmitted about Israel is examined and analysed, every conceivable connotation, real or imaginary, explored, to try to discover the motive of the writer or film producer. 'Is he for us or against us?' And one quality which all Israelis share is a lack of inhibition about saying precisely what's on their minds.

Not many Israelis will agree with the political views of Uri Avnery – a former member of the Knesset, the parliament of the Jewish state, and an anti-Establishment figure who advocates dialogue with the PLO. But I suspect that most Israelis and probably most Jews would agree with the sentiments which he expressed on the opening pages of *Israel Without Zionists*, a book about the Jewish state: 'I don't pretend to be objective about Israel, I don't believe anyone is, or can be. There is something in the air of our country that leads to extremes . . . Today nearly everything written about Israel is propaganda.'

It's not just Israel – the same could be said of nearly everything published about the Arab countries, too. The whole region breeds extremes. And it was on the basis of many years of observing and reporting on the two sides in the Middle East conflict as they retreated into 'extreme' positions that I decided to write this book. I wanted, in particular, to look at Israel as a state in the Middle East, to see how it has changed since the early days of European-inspired pioneering Zionism, and how it has absorbed many of the characteristics and attitudes of the region – something which, in my experience, the Jewish community outside Israel often finds difficult to accept. But this process, as we shall see, has not narrowed the gap between the extremes in the Middle East – indeed, quite the opposite.

Uri Avnery says that propagandists see Israel as 'either a holy place, full of upright pioneers, heroic warriors and virtuous maidens, or . . . a den of robbers, cruel adventurers and shameless women, who have fallen upon an innocent people and raped a country.' I think he is right, and that is why 'a state in the Middle East' is my point of departure. This book risks upsetting Jews and Arabs equally by deliberately ignoring the rights and wrongs of the process which led to the creation of the Jewish state in 1948. In my opinion, far too many books and other publications are influenced in their approach to Israel by their perception of history. In that steamy atmosphere the luxuriant foliage of the myth flourishes, obscuring some basic truths on both sides of the Middle East conflict.

This is not a history book, it is a book about Israel today. But it is not a textbook or a reference book – rather, it is a record of observations, both my own and those of the Israelis themselves, presented against the backcloth of the Middle East. Because it is not a textbook I make no apology for the fact that – for example – while I talk of 'the kibbutz movement', I do not dwell on its origins, its history and its ideological splits. Anyone who knows Israel well will not need to be told; and to spell it out in detail is to risk losing the attention of those whose knowledge of the Jewish state is less broad and may well be clouded by myth and prejudice. In other words, I hope to make Israel more accessible and easier to understand for those on the outside, but at the same time I don't pretend that I am presenting a comprehensive history.

Many of the issues which are discussed in the coming pages will be considered 'negative' by lovers of Israel. 'I hope', an Israeli acquaintance remarked on hearing of my plans to write a book, 'that it's not going to be yet another one dumping on Israel.' Another Israeli was even blunter: 'Is it going to be anti-Semitic?' But this is neither a guidebook to the Jewish state nor an apologia for it. The rich cultural life of Israel, the country's success in 'turning the deserts green' and other achievements of the Jewish state are well documented, and acknowledging them is not the purpose of this book. Equally, to point out, as the Arabs might prefer it, that forests and parks have been created on land where Palestinian villages once stood, and that tens of thousands of Palestinians have spent the past forty years and more living in squalid refugee camps, is not the purpose, either. Such subjects have been well documented and commented upon elsewhere.

A nation which has returned to land granted to it by God and to which the Arabs never had a true claim? Or, perhaps, as the Arabs would say, a cancer in the heart of the Middle East? The challenge is to write a book about Israel which shows the nation as any other in the world would like to be shown: without the observer being blinkered by historical, cultural or religious prejudice.

Viewed in this way, Israel emerges as a state of great complexity. For Westerners, this picture is sometimes both surprising and disturbing. The challenge for the Middle East (Arabs and Jews alike) and for the world outside must be to come to terms with an Israel viewed from this uncluttered perspective.

CHAPTER ONE

———— • ◆ • ————

View from the inside

MOST Israelis probably don't hear it any more. A subconscious mechanism filters it out. But if your ear is not tuned like that of an Israeli you're liable to be disturbed frequently, day or night, by the menacing shriek and rumble of air force jets criss-crossing in a matter of seconds the tight band of airspace over Israel and Israeli-controlled territory. Window panes regularly rattle and buildings shudder as the sharp crack of a sonic boom echoes across the city. A newcomer will rush to the window to look for the smoke, convinced that it is a bomb. But on the street outside there will be nothing out of the ordinary to see.

The Israelis, like the Lebanese, have developed a keen intuitive sense of what constitutes danger. Both peoples are addicts of news bulletins. In office blocks in Israel, even in the lifts, it is common to hear news broadcasts relayed over loudspeaker systems. And both peoples have developed an alarm mechanism when they see or sense things out of the ordinary. Like a suspicious parcel left outside a shop, like the sight of people in the street suddenly running. Or like the sound of a bomb exploding.

I thought I had been away from Lebanon too long. The sonic booms in Israel had fooled me so often that I didn't trust my judgement in distinguishing one explosion from another. But there was no mistaking the deep, dull texture of that particular one. I was talking on the phone at the time, and I glanced at my wife Lynne. She had clearly had the same reaction.

Within minutes the night was filled by blue and red flashing lights of police vehicles and ambulances, and a crescendo of sirens. Groups of people appeared from the buildings round about, some hurrying towards the site of the explosion. The police were cordoning off streets and diverting traffic. As the last bus was allowed past, the passengers were crowded at the windows. Outside, the crowd's surge forward continued. Bystanders offered their opinions: 'A bomb on a bus.' 'A hand-grenade under a bus.' 'I saw a flash from just beyond that white van,' a youth in a T-shirt said in an American accent.

It turned out to be nothing worth reporting: a relatively small charge under a parked van. No one injured, very little damage. But the adrenalin in the crowd was flowing and they were in no mood to disperse. It was inevitable that the chant would start: 'Death to Arabs! Death to Arabs!'

As I walked home along streets still clear of traffic the television news was in mid-bulletin, and its sound was pouring out into the night in unison from a thousand open windows. Many people were out on their balconies staring in the direction of the blast. And for a moment that blur of images – of emergency vehicles, television lights and people with strained, anxious, angry faces – transported me back to Beirut and what could have been one of a score of similar occasions. Only the chant of the angry crowd was different: 'Death to Israel! Death to Zionism!' Two sides of the same soiled Middle Eastern coin.

Israelis face a daily task of trying to pretend that life is normal when circumstances indicate quite the opposite. The Middle East conflict casts a shadow over Israel as much as it does over Syria or Jordan. The speck of a high-flying aircraft over northern Israel chalking wide circles in the clear blue autumn sky may be a pretty sight, but the purpose of the airborne reconnaissance is just as serious as similar missions trailing vapour over Syria or Jordan. From any of these planes you have a clear view of the whole area of conflict.

Inside 'fortress Israel', as much as in the surrounding fortress states of the Arab world, the civilian population finds itself inextricably linked to the military machine. Convoys of tank transporters lumber slowly up the roads on both the Israeli and Syrian slopes of the Golan Heights where a United Nations buffer force monitors the movements of each army. Military roads are cut purposefully through the Samarian hills to enable quick mobilization from Israel's coastal population centres to the Jordanian front in the east. With exactly the same precision, military roads are cut from Syria across the border into Lebanon to allow unhindered access for tanks and other heavy equipment.

Separating civilian life from military life is difficult in a country where the army is the people's army. At any one time reservists make up about two-thirds of the Israelis in uniform. School-leavers (with some notable exceptions, whom we'll meet later) are required to do army duty; for the women it is two years, for the men three. Thereafter, the men are liable for annual reserve duty, which can last for a month or more, until they are fifty-five. This is a national duty and is recognized as such by the overwhelming majority of the population. There are few dissenters, but many grumblers. Army duty in all its aspects – the unpredictability of the timing, the dangers, the disruption to business and family life – places a great burden on Israelis.

Hundreds of thousands of Israelis have spent at least part of their time in the reserves in the West Bank and Gaza Strip, the territories which Israel captured (respectively from Jordan and Egypt) in the Middle East War of 1967. Since 9 December 1987 military service in the Occupied Territories has taken on a new, and for most people a very ugly, dimension: confrontation with a Palestinian population engaged in a violent struggle to put an end to the occupation. Beyond question, soldiers face dangers: rocks and fire-bombs are thrown by young Palestinians with the intention of harming the Israeli security forces. But every soldier knows, too, that it is an uneven contest. And the casualty figures are proof of this: many hundreds of Palestinians killed, as against a handful of Israeli soldiers. Being the superior protagonist in an uneven contest can have its problems, too. A teenager who has recently put on uniform for the first time might find himself with a loaded automatic rifle in an alien and hostile environment, facing a crowd which is spitting hatred at him. Sometimes he'll panic and pull the trigger. Wilful excesses have at times been committed by Israeli troops (sometimes from the crack brigades whose training has been geared towards fighting a conventional war, not acting as a policeman in a civilian rebellion) when confronting the uprising in the territories. Some incidents of brutality and harassment have been investigated by the Israeli military authorities, countless others have never even been reported. But fear is a predominant emotion among young soldiers and police as they face angry crowds, fear of the almost tangible atmosphere of hatred and alienation, almost as much as of the stone or petrol bomb.

These confrontations have become routine. So have the reports of the resulting casualties. There's a limit to how long one can be shocked, of course. The inevitable outcome, it seems to me, is an indifference to the taking of human life. In 1989 new rules of engagement were announced by the army, under which Palestinian youths with their faces masked by the traditional head-dress, the kaffiyeh, were to be considered in the same category as any person endangering the life of a soldier. In other words, if, after warning shots had been fired, the individual did not give himself up, the soldier had the right to open fire, aiming below the knee. The number of masked youths shot and killed rose considerably in the weeks that followed – not shot below the knee, but in the head and chest, sometimes while running away. The army says that the circumstances of every death are investigated. That may be the case. But what was striking at the time was the absence of any public questioning of the fact that soldiers, sometimes under difficult circumstances but sometimes too in broad daylight, were killing people when the order clearly stated that shots should be aimed below the knee.

'In the Casbah district of Nablus last night,' Israel Radio reported one day early in 1990, 'an Arab youth was shot dead by soldiers after he failed to obey an order to stop. An initial investigation showed that he was suspected of being a member of a local shock committee.' End of item. No mention of lives being in danger. No certainty even of the youth's identity and guilt.

Israelis say, when I raise such points, that correspondents and other foreigners spend too long dwelling on the small details of behaviour in the Occupied Territories while ignoring the wholesale brutality that Arab regimes use to silence opposition and dissent. What about Syria, what about Lebanon, what about Iraq, and so on? There is certainly a wide gap between Israel and some of the surrounding Arab states in terms of the number of lives lost in the suppression of dissent. But, it seems to me, oppressive regimes survive in an atmosphere in which there is a callous indifference to the value of human life. And something of that indifference is appearing in Israel. 'Why', I asked an Israeli who fought in the battles for the creation of the state, 'do you think there isn't more of an outcry about the number of deaths in the Occupied Territories?' His reply: 'It just shows the level to which we have sunk.'

'I did not come to Israel', one father wrote in a letter to the papers, 'to have my son kill women and children.' 'We know', an American-born professor at the Hebrew University of Jerusalem, told me, 'that in two years' time our son will be in the army. Chances are, he'll be in a combat unit, and I believe that serving in the Israeli army today is immoral.'

'This whole façade, this whole joke of civil disobedience, of using rocks and Molotov cocktails – it seems to me the whole world is anti-Semitic, and they colour over and whitewash what the Arabs do, and every time a Jew does something in self-defence this becomes a major catastrophe.' The speaker is an ultra-orthodox Jew, another American by birth, living in the Old City of Jerusalem. For him, army action isn't tough enough.

Make peace with the Palestinians and give them their own state alongside Israel. Or expel them. These are extreme views, and they represent minority thinking, but they are views which can be heard in the Knesset, Israel's 120-seat Parliament; they are views the large, silent majority is hearing every day. By and large, most Israelis seem to think that neither extreme position is realistic, and nothing in between seems to offer much hope. 'There is no solution,' a stall-holder told me as he served customers in the Mahane Yehuda market in Jerusalem. His family emigrated to Israel in the early 1950s from Iran. Against a background of a fundamental distrust of politicians and the political system, and evidence of increasing polarization between left and right, many Israelis I know simply throw up their hands and say: something will happen. Fatalism, that crippling Middle Eastern disease, is spreading in Israel.

In the spring of 1989 the Israeli Prime Minister, Mr Yitzhak Shamir, went to Washington to discuss with American leaders the prospects for starting a Middle East peace process. Before he left I recorded a dozen or more random street interviews. Not one person, even supporters of the Prime Minister's Likud party, had the slightest confidence in the ability of Mr Shamir to achieve a breakthrough.

As one pioneer who fought for the creation of the state commented: 'We're all pessimistic about Shamir's chances or anyone else's. But what's worrying is that we're all becoming fatalistic, too – even the Ashkenazim [the Jews from Europe and America].'

The distinction between Ashkenazis and Sephardis (Jews from Oriental countries), which was once clear and marked in Israeli society, is gradually disappearing because of intermarriage and better opportunities for the Oriental community. According to figures from Haifa University, about 20 per cent of all marriages in Israel bring couples together from the two communities. Professor Arnon Soffer, an expert at Haifa University on demographic trends, has seen the intertwining of the two within his own family. 'My family is from Russia,' he told me. 'My daughter is a third-generation Israeli, of Russian descent. Her boy-friend is an Israeli whose parents came from Algeria. He was born here. Both my daughter and her boy-friend are pure Israelis – "Sabras" – regardless of their different family backgrounds.'

The distinction between the two communities was most marked in the early years of the Jewish state when there was mass immigration from the Arab countries of North Africa, and from Yemen, Iraq and Iran. For decades the Sephardis felt inferior outsiders in the young Israeli nation. David Krivine of the *Jerusalem Post* newspaper explained: 'The system into which the Sephardi immigrants had been "absorbed" was a good one, but it had one big fault: the negligible Sephardi hand in creating it. The prevailing way of life carried the Ashkenazi hallmark. It did not belong to the settlers from the Middle East and North Africa; it was not rooted in their culture.'

Today, the Sephardi community, far from feeling inferior and excluded, is a dominant and growing force within the mainstream of Israeli society. In fact it is gradually putting its stamp on that society. One can still find what Professor Soffer calls 'some islands where the Sephardi community live in isolation, some depressed areas,' but Jews of Oriental backgrounds are today confident and self-assured. They came of age in the 1977 general elections when they helped the Likud bloc led by Menachem Begin win power. Up to that election Labour had led all Israel's governments. It seemed almost the birthright of Labour, with its roots in the European democratic and socialist traditions, to hold the reins of government.

The strong influence of the Sephardi community on the political scene over recent years reflects their strength within society. Professor Soffer's office is high up in the skyscraper tower which dominates Haifa University, which in turn dominates the skyline of Mount Carmel. Professor Soffer pointed down to the Carmel district below, with its comfortable houses and luxury hotels, as an example of one district in Israel which is completely 'Western'-oriented. The Professor's family lives there. 'Of course,' he said, 'we, in areas like this, are losing power. The natural increase in the size of the community of "Western" Jews is very low. In Haifa and Tel Aviv there's almost zero growth. The growth of the population among Jews from Middle Eastern countries is more than one and a half times that among "Western" Jews. On top of this, many "Western"-oriented secular Israelis are leaving the country.'

In an article in the *Jerusalem Quarterly*, Professor Soffer spelled out his

19

views in the following way: 'Any attempt to argue that the rate of emigration is not growing is statistical hoodwinking. In the past the leavers were mainly recent immigrants who found it difficult to become acclimatized, whereas nowadays the majority of the emigrants are Israeli-born, university-educated, many of them engineers and scientists. They are usually part of the Israel Defence Force's officer corps and have a share in building the quality of Israeli society.'

Professor Soffer believes that, as a whole, Israeli society is moving slowly and surely 'to the East', and he cites in support of this the fatalism that one finds increasingly among Israelis, as well as such things as the behaviour of people and the aggressive and erratic way in which they drive their cars.

Another headache is the demographic balance between Jews and non-Jews. If one were to assume that the West Bank and Gaza Strip will remain under Israeli control (as many, if not the majority, of Israelis would like), then projections of what that balance would look like in the year 2000 show the non-Jewish population (Palestinians with Israeli citizenship inside Israel, plus Palestinians in the Occupied Territories) fast catching up with the Jewish one. In 1987 the balance was 62 per cent Jew against 38 per cent non-Jew. By the end of the century the equivalent figures would be around 55 and 45 per cent.

Looking at current trends, Professor Soffer says: 'The demographic problem constitutes the paramount danger to the foundation of the Jewish-Zionist state.' However, precisely because it is the Jewish state, trends here are affected by trends outside. It's 'less a question of people being pulled to Israel, and more one of people being pushed here.' The arrival of an enormous number of Russians, for example (40,000 between January and June 1990, with predictions that the eventual total could be more than a million), is changing the pattern considerably in terms of the numerical balance between Jews and non-Jews. Some right-wing Israelis are confident that the sudden influx of Soviet Jewry has overcome the demography problem. Indeed, they say, far from being afraid to annex the West Bank and Gaza Strip for fear of the Jewish population being swamped by non-Jews, Israel must hold on to those territories to make room for the new arrivals. The more interesting question is: to what extent will the arrival of Russians, from an environment where freedom of speech, democracy and free enterprise are unknown, halt the unquantifiable Eastward-moving trend within Israeli society? Indications are that the traditionally right-wing Soviet Jews could bolster support for those political groups which are hostile to Arabs and suspicious of them, too. So while the demographic pattern is changing, the drift towards more aggressive 'Middle East-style' attitudes may be accelerated when the Russians become Israelis.

There is today a certain identifiable 'Israeli' look among the incredible range of faces and skins which make up the inhabitants of the Jewish state. The young Israeli man is tall and slim, and athletic in his looks and his movements. His hair is dark and coarse, worn cropped closely to his head, and his skin is the rich olive colour that you find throughout the Middle East. Walking one evening in Jerusalem, I saw a group of young soldiers in uniform, but off duty, coming down Ben Yehuda street, a pedestrian-only thoroughfare in the centre of the Jewish half of the city. With their dark skins and their jaunty, confident manner, they reminded me of an almost identical scene from a previous year. The look and the mood of the soldiers in my memory had been strikingly similar. The only difference was: they had been Syrian soldiers, striding down the main street in the Hamadiya Suq in Damascus.

The music that you hear in Ben Yehuda street in Jerusalem will probably be Western in influence. But you need only take a five-minute walk to Mahane Yehuda market to hear the distinctive quarter-tone of Arabic music that the Sephardi community has brought into Israeli culture. That music has arrived, but it does not make frequent appearance in the showcases of Israeli culture. The world outside respects and admires the excellence of Israeli orchestras and classical musicians. Orchestral concerts in Jerusalem, Tel Aviv and Haifa have the same atmosphere as similar occasions in London, Paris or New York. They are an important element in the musical fabric of Israel, and so is Western pop music. But to regard either as representative of the taste of the overwhelming majority of Israelis is as wrong as the common assumption overseas that 'all Israelis speak English'. Israel is not an extension of Brooklyn or Golders Green, even though links with such communities may still be strong.

Young Israelis recognize the existence of these links as well as anyone in the country. They may enjoy Western music and may copy Western styles of fashion. Turn on Israel Radio or Army Radio and there's a good chance you'll hear a British or American pop song. However, the output of a radio station does not necessarily reflect the taste or wishes of its listeners. Little surprise, then, to find, in a survey conducted by the Ministry of Education and quoted by the *Jerusalem Post*, that 'while Israelis of all ages have no objection to listening to the international hit parade, the majority would prefer the lyrics in Hebrew . . . and they would like to have more of a Middle Eastern flavour in songs originating from Israel.' The Ministry also heard complaints from Israelis from North Africa that while Western-style pop music was presented on radio as 'Israeli', Middle Eastern music was called 'ethnic'. Some months later the Education Minister Yitzhak Navon said there was a need for a more visible Sephardi presence on Israel Television; the public needed to see more faces with which it could 'identify ethnically'.

The question of whether Israel is more a 'Western' or more an 'Eastern' state is not new. Israel has always been a melting-pot. By definition it is home to Jews from all over the world. Because it is situated in the Middle East it is caught up in all the problems of that region. And because a large and fast-growing section of the population also has its roots in the region it should be little surprise that Israel is taking on a more Middle Eastern complexion. Indeed I believe that to fail to realize this fact, or to choose to ignore it (as many people in Europe and the United States appear to do), is to wish on Israel features which once dominated its character but today no longer do so. More important still, to see Israel as a state fitting increasingly comfortably into the region is to go a long way towards understanding why Israelis, politicians and public alike, act as they do.

The adoption of attitudes that are indigenous to the region is a gradual process. Doubtless for years to come Israel will at times seem more Western, at times more Middle Eastern. On occasions, too, it will seem a contradictory mixture of both. Take, for example, the following extract from a news item in the *Jerusalem Post* of September 1989:

'Don't drink or wade in the water at the lion fountain opposite the Liberty Bell Garden, Jerusalem district health officer Alex Levinthal warned this week. 'The fountain is not meant for wading, swimming or drinking,' Levinthal said.

Lab tests have found potentially dangerous bacteria in the water . . .

'The fountain is for looking at, and children may sit on the lions,' he said. 'Nowhere else in the Western world are decorative fountains turned into swimming pools. But in our Middle Eastern, multi-ethnic culture, people are not aware that this is dangerous.'

Two short sentences combine the two elements, 'Western world' and 'Middle Eastern, multi-ethnic culture'. Israelis are scarcely aware of this contradiction, just as they learn to ignore the scream of jets streaking across their skies day and night and just as the Sephardi-Ashkenazi distinction is fading in the minds of the young. Foreigners, too, are not always aware of the changes that have been taking place. Many Europeans and Americans, in my experience, see Israel as an extension of the West, both in outward trappings and attitudes. The fact that Israel happens to be situated in the Middle East, the thinking goes, merely points up the Western (and therefore superior) character of the state when matched against those surrounding it. Such apparent logic does an injustice to Israel and leaves the door open for gross misunderstandings of how the country thinks and acts. On two occasions while in Israel I was criticized in abusive terms by members of visiting delegations of the Board of Jewish Deputies in Britain. Their objections to my reporting (and that of British journalists in Israel in general) was clearly based on an image of Israel that took no account of the social changes of recent years. And the critics did not want to be told that such changes had taken place.

There are many aspects of Israeli life and sections of the Israeli community that are still entrenched in Western traditions. Towns and settlements spawn shops and office blocks which would not look out of place in any European population centre. It is also a fact, though, that large sections of the Israeli public understand little English and speak none; it is one of the surprises that many outsiders find when they arrive. Not really so surprising as you get to know the place and see the demographic pattern. And the confusion exists not just in the minds of goyim, or non-Jews. 'I don't like the way the Israeli children turn out,' the Jewish wife of an American correspondent in Jerusalem told me. 'They're rude and arrogant. But I guess one can keep one's Western standards.'

To hear a suggestion that Israel abides by anything but 'Western standards' would be in itself a shock to many people. The Israel of the post-1967 Middle East War era seemed, to many millions of people in the West, the apogee of what Western governments would like to display in the way of confidence and self-assurance, had they only the nerve. This was the era which followed the six days in June 1967 when 'tiny Israel' crushed the collective might of the Arab world, the era which saw the brilliantly daring and successful rescue of hostages held on an airliner in

Entebbe in 1976, the clinical bombing of a nuclear reactor in Iraq thousands of miles away in the heart of enemy territory in 1981, the destruction of Syria's air defence system in 1982 and the launching of a rocket into space in 1988. Little wonder that Israel's image as a highly motivated but also technologically advanced state took root around the world. Not least in the Arab states.

Newcomers to Israel frequently express shock at the dilapidated state of much of the infrastructure – like the creaking telephone system and the shoddy state of many public buildings. On top of the ever-growing burden of defence spending has come a lust for consumer products that has drained both the public and private purse. The loser has been the infrastructure. In 1988 the whole of the population aged less than forty years old was ordered to be vaccinated against polio following an outbreak in several parts of the country. The source of the outbreak was untreated sewage which in at least one town was found flowing down the street. The country's sewerage system in a good number of localities, it turned out, was both antiquated and in serious need of repair. The Health Ministry and the Interior Ministry (the body responsible for sewerage) swapped accusations of blame for the outbreak. But the controversy was allowed to fade, and nothing, as far as anyone was aware, was done to tackle the root of the problem.

On a daily basis one comes up against the counterbalances of Israel's technological achievements. Telephoning Tel Aviv from Jerusalem (a distance of some forty miles) can be a major problem. Household fixtures and fittings tend to be shoddy and badly made. The electrical wall-sockets in the twenty-year-old house where I lived would come out of the wall whenever one tried to take out a plug. 'Israelis like to feel they're a modern, outgoing race,' a recent immigrant from Britain told me; 'they've invented a lot of things and have contributed a great deal to certain areas of technology. But the administration and bureaucracy is very Third-World. They've got much to offer, but also they've got a lot to learn in terms of quality control and reliability.'

The education and health services are seriously underfunded. Money for university research is scarce, prompting some of the best brains in Israel to look for positions abroad. The Centre for Policy Research in Israel reported towards the end of 1989 that 'the amount of research conducted by Israelis abroad has increased greatly during recent years. This may increase the rate of emigration from Israel of young scientists and cause major damage to the future of science here . . . The primary reasons why young Israeli scientists conduct their research abroad are research conditions, employment possibilities, economic reasons, political reasons and the quality of life.' And, at the lower end of the education scale, dwindling budgets have forced thousands of Israeli parents to resort to contributing out of their own pockets to pay for private tuition or to contribute to a kitty to be paid to a teacher to enable him to give extra classes.

In Europe or the United States such inadequacies would be the stuff of political debate. Elections would be won or lost on issues of this kind. But in Israel security is so much the dominant issue in the daily life of both the state and the individual that domestic matters simply do not become election issues. To the horror of Israelis who worry about the deterioration of the country's infrastructure, neither health, nor education nor any other social issue gets a mention. Part of the reason for this, too, lies in the electoral system. Because votes are distributed on a proportional representation system members of the Knesset have no constituency to whom they must account; and conversely the constituents have no channel into which they can direct their complaints.

Parliamentary democracy in Israel is imperfect; but it has survived, despite the arrival of hundreds of thousands of Jews from countries where there was no democratic tradition. These arrivals, though, have given the democratic process a flavour which is unique to Israel. And compared with the rest of the Middle East, Israel certainly is a democracy.

Whether or not the fault lies in the imperfection of the democracy, Israelis are never short of something to complain about. 'This last year has not been an easy one for the state of Israel. We have had to face difficult trials and situations.' The speaker was President Chaim Herzog in an address to the nation on the occasion of the Jewish new year of 5750 (in September 1989). 'This time the battle is hard,' the Prime Minister Yitzhak Shamir had said a few months earlier. 'It's a miracle that, thus far, we have held our own against the world where no element supports our position.'

One of the first things that a new arrival in Israel must do is buy electric plugs which are of a design that I've never seen anywhere else. On one of my first days there I went into the hardware shop, scooped up a couple of dozen plugs and went to the counter. 'Why so many?' the man inquired.

'I've just arrived.'

'Welcome to Israel,' he continued, assuming I was a new immigrant and adding with a chuckle: 'It's not easy, believe me.'

His words puzzled me. But it wasn't long before I began to understand. 'Life is hard,' was the predominant message from the dozens of Israelis I was to meet during my three-year stay. It involves the difficulties of making ends meet; the stress of living in a state that feels itself small, isolated and unloved in a hostile world and in a particularly hostile region; the constant anxiety that there will be another war or another terrorist attack; the social strain and economic disruption caused by army reserve duty; and constant political uncertainty.

Such stresses inevitably leave their mark on Israelis. On the first day back in Israel after a holiday abroad, I was driving to work and it suddenly hit me how unhappy everyone around me looked. Israelis, by their own admission, are rude and aggressive to each other and to foreigners alike. An American student who's lived in Israel for many years told me that Israelis 'think less about other people even than in New York. I remember going back to New York and finding everything less tense.' This lack of consideration for others (or, as an Israeli immigrant from Canada defined it, 'This lack of treating each other nicely on a day-to-day basis') finds expression on the roads, in the queue at the supermarket or the bank, in the bus – everywhere. And it is reflected in the nation's humour – or lack of it.

Discovering that the Jewish state has not inherited the richness of Jewish humour was a major surprise. I attended the 'Third International Conference on Jewish Humour' at Tel Aviv University, to which delegates (academics and 'humour analysts') came from nine countries. Not surprisingly the United States, where Jewish humour blossomed, was well represented. American delegates may well have been concerned to hear that one of the best known and most endearing aspects of the Jewish character has not taken root in Israel.

In one session at the conference politics was discussed. 'Humour', the young researcher reported, 'has no part in the make-up of political charisma in Israel.' Indeed the unwritten rule among politicians precludes the following topics as subjects for jokes: sex, love affairs, spouses of members of the Knesset, the army, the presidents of Israel, health, body defects, age, Nazi Germany, religion, death, and sports. Political satire, the bread-and-butter of fringe theatre around the world, is not usually part of the Israeli humour diet either. A newspaper report looking ahead to the 1989 Acre Fringe festival tried to tempt audiences by declaring that it would be the biggest 'and least controversial' thus far. And in case there was any room left for doubt, the organizers 'stressed' that productions 'would deal primarily with history, the Bible and the Holocaust'.

An explanation for the lack of humour came from Professor Avner Ziv of the School of Education at Tel Aviv University. He draws a clear distinction between the Jews of the Diaspora and those of Israel. The former developed the humour of the minority; it was self-mocking and never very aggressive. 'When we came here we wanted to develop "a new Jew", and we did it. He's strong, he feels himself almost like a superman, he's sure of everything. And people who're sure of everything don't have much humour. We're so convinced we're great that we've forgotten to laugh at ourselves. The result is that Israeli humour is like the Israeli – aggressive, quick and arrogant.' The commonest subjects of joke in Israel, it emerges, are ethnic groups (Arabs and Israelis of Arab origin seem to suffer the most), puns on the Hebrew language, insults pertaining to a Knesset member's intelligence or personality, and money matters.

Israel can argue with justification that as a state it needs to take an aggressive stance to be ready for the potential military challenge from the Arab world. Many Israelis, including the Prime Minister Mr Shamir, see the uprising in the Occupied Territories as simply an extension of that long-running conflict, which in turn is part of the Jews' battle for survival. Furthermore, their argument goes, because the world at large does not appreciate either the magnitude of the threat or Israel's distrust of international guarantees of security, Israelis have no choice but to act in their own interests. Frequently therefore, decisions or actions are taken which are regarded by the international community as baffling or stubbornly obtuse. 'We don't welcome isolation,' Mr Shamir said in one of those statements which characterize the most defiant and stubborn of Israeli politicians. 'It is perhaps our historical destiny to swim against the tide. But we keep on swimming, we have not yet drowned.'

It is a subject for debate whether such an attitude is the product of introversion conditioned by centuries of persecution and suffering, or of arrogant and thick-skinned self-centredness ('We act as though we're the centre of the universe and no one else exists,' one Israeli told me). It's probably both.

The insecurity which the horrors of the Holocaust instilled in the Jewish people is still alive in Israel. Hundreds of thousands of families in Israel lost relatives in the Holocaust; equally many thousands, from Arab and African countries, had no direct experience of it. Nevertheless the Holocaust experience is central to the education process in Israel, and no opportunity is missed to remind the younger generations of the appalling atrocities committed by the Nazis. The trial of the Nazi war criminal John Demjanjuk in Jerusalem was held in a specially converted hall and broadcast on radio and television for this reason as much as any other.

Each year on Holocaust Memorial Day Israelis remember the millions of Jews who were killed by the Nazis. For two minutes, as sirens wail across the country, life comes to a halt. One year I looked out of my office window at this moment. The traffic stopped; one young man I noticed walked out of an office block and then stood to attention in the middle of the street. He wore a blue T-shirt, jeans, a blue kippa (the skullcap which is obligatory for observant Jews), and a pistol in a holster attached to his belt. Guns are everywhere in Israel – automatic rifles carried by soldiers, both on and off duty, and pistols in holsters or tucked into waistbands. According to Professor Simha Landau of the Institute of Criminology, 'there are over 200,000 licensed weapons in private hands . . . This indicates that we feel far less secure than ever before, and also increases the potential for violence.'

Israelis feel misunderstood by the world. They believe the international community stood by and did nothing as Jews were being taken to the gas ovens in Germany and Poland, and that the world can never fully understand the shadow which the Holocaust casts over their lives. And another frequently recurring theme in the interviews carried out for this book was that the world fails to understand the dangers which Israel faces today. Most of the reporting by foreign correspondents either based in Israel or visiting the country is regarded as being biased and inaccurate. On some occasions there may be justification in this view. But more often than not, in my experience, accusations of bias are based on the philosophy: if you are not for us, then you are against us. In other words, reporting of Israel that shows the country in anything but the best light is regarded as 'hostile'. Israelis are fiercely defensive in the face of criticism. The same goes very often for the Palestinians and other Arabs. Indeed, in reporting the Middle East conflict one is reporting events against historical perspectives that are interpreted often in ways that are diametrically opposed. 'Objective' reporting means to each side viewing current developments through the historical perspective (or bias) of that particular side.

Yoav Biran, Israel's Ambassador in London, said in a published interview that he had seen some cases in the British media where he believed there was 'an exaggerated interest in exposing the negative and overlooking the positive aspects of Israel'. But he was quick to add that he wasn't asking journalists to judge Israel by the standards which are applied to the Arab world. 'It would be a sad day for Israel were they to use the same criteria.'

This is the point: does one judge Israel by European or Middle Eastern standards? The answer must be: somewhere in between. But without question, while Israel has a press that is freer than any other in the region, if there was any change in the three years I spent in Israel it was in the direction of freedoms being eroded rather than expanded. There were many examples of abuse and violence being directed at journalists, Israeli and foreign, and official restrictions being imposed on them. An accredited correspondent with a London paper who was accused (and only accused) of having violated censorship regulations was subjected to lengthy harassment every time she entered or left the country. This included strip searches and the photocopying of all her notes and private papers. Such heavy-handed tactics are characteristic of countries with which Israel would definitely not welcome comparisons.

No Israeli would countenance any close comparison between his country and an Arab state. Indeed, in talking to scores of Israelis from many backgrounds I discovered a widespread, deep dislike and a deep distrust of Arabs. Many, possibly most, of the people who expressed these views had had little, if any, direct contact with Arabs on which to base their opinions. It is a deep-rooted prejudice, noticeable more in the younger generations than the old, and lamented only by that small section of society which espouses (unfashionable) liberal and humanitarian values.

An Israeli whom I got to know had emigrated from America nine years previously with his wife and three children. In this time the parents had watched their seven-year-old American son become an Israeli teenager. The parents are not altogether happy with what they've seen. On the credit side the father noticed all his children taking a greater interest in politics and world events than they would have done in the United States. In that family, like in every other in Israel, basic issues of war and peace are the staple diet of conversation. But the parents, who class themselves as left-of-centre liberals, have also watched their son adopt the attitudes of his school fellows – attitudes they describe as being based on extremes. The young 'see issues of Arabs and Jews in black-and-white terms. It is a form of prejudice, of bigotry, that's typical of the young generation. They're part of a society that's mixed up with history and hatred. In that sense our son is now Middle Eastern . . . to us it's kind of sad.'

Recent general elections have borne out opinion-poll findings of a gradual shift by young voters towards political parties on the right, against a background of increasing polarization. The right-wing parties, by and large, are the most chauvinistically nationalist in their outlook, and least tolerant of Arabs. A passionate hatred of Arabs simmers only a little way below the surface calm on many of the streets of Israel's cities. Acts of violence perpetrated by Arabs against Jews immediately trigger indiscriminate and vicious acts of revenge against anyone in the vicinity unfortunate enough to be taken as an Arab. I witnessed one such ugly scene of crowd hysteria on Jaffa Road, the main thoroughfare of west Jerusalem, after a Palestinian had run amok with a knife, killing three people and wounding several more. 'The appearance of uncontrollable crowd passions in that fraction of a second – it's a sign of how we're becoming more and more part of the Middle East.' That was how one senior Israeli diplomat assessed matters.

His words brought to mind the sudden explosions of street anger into terrifying riots which I witnessed in Syria and Jordan as a child in the 1950s, and later as an adult in Egypt and elsewhere in the Middle East. But I hear a much stronger echo of those societies in the degree of hatred that ordinary people on both sides of the conflict show for each other. Many Arabs I've met can't perceive an Israeli as being anything other than a member of an alien nation which has usurped part of the Arab homeland; furthermore, they believe it's only a matter of time before his 'expansionist tendencies' lead him to conquer more Arab land. Conversely, many Israelis believe all Arabs have one basic intention, regardless of what they may say in public: to drive Israel into the sea.

Insecurity combined with blind prejudice, it is true, plays a big part in the formation of these attitudes. The upshot is undeniably depressing. The Middle East character has many good qualities; tolerance, compassion, and the promotion of liberal and humanitarian value, are not, unfortunately, foremost among them.

Public pronouncements on both sides of the Middle East conflict are sometimes strikingly similar in tone and phraseology. This is an extract from a statement broadcast by the PLO Central Radio in Baghdad in April 1989: 'This terrorist operation against the people of the Intifada is a link within the chain of Zionist terror against the Palestinian people which has been escalating since Shamir's recent visit to Washington. While the Israeli terrorist operations against our people . . . have not stopped for one moment, Israel's escalation of its crimes against our people has increased, inflicting casualties among them every day. This has transformed the practices of the Zionist terrorists into continuous massacres aimed at wiping out the Palestinian people . . .'

In the following month, the Israeli Foreign Minister Moshe Arens, speaking on Israel Radio, had this to say about the PLO Chairman, Yasser Arafat: 'We are talking about a man who heads a terrorist organization that is responsible for the worst horrors the world has witnessed since the end of World War Two . . . Over the past few weeks the Territories have been experiencing a wave of terror led by the PLO. This time the terror is directed at the Palestinians themselves. They stab people, axe them to pieces, burn them . . .'

It would be surprising, surely, if Israel did not gradually identify with at least some aspects of its surroundings. At the very basic level, Israelis have largely adopted the food of the Middle East (hummous, pitta bread, strained yoghurt, olives) as being more suited to the climate and the environment than the heavy dishes of Eastern Europe where much of the population originally had its roots. Many words of Arabic have been adopted into everyday colloquial Hebrew. And while the Israeli air force patrols the skies day and night, and the army patrols the borders, physical barriers can't stop the flow of regional influences. People in Israel breathe the same air as people in the neighbouring states, and it would be odd if the whiff of religious fundamentalism that is detectable in Egypt and Jordan, for example, were not discernible in Israel. On top of all its other troubles, Israel has to watch for the spread of religious fanaticism among both its Jewish and Arab communities. In the Middle East the tendency to seek solace in one's traditional religious roots is often an expression of protest and despair. And the religions in the region are most certainly not by-words for liberal ideas and tolerance.

The degree to which the Jewish religion should or should not influence daily life in the Jewish state has been an issue since Israel was created. Should Israel strive to be a Torah-studying nation awaiting the coming of the Messiah, or should the aim simply be to keep alive a nation that can be a homeland and a refuge for people who are Jews, both secular and religious? Religious Jews feel that the secular influence of the state is too strong; secular Israelis feel increasingly choked by the growing power and influence of the observant community.

The Israelis' view from within is complicated and confusing. And all the time there is the underlying fear that the fortress state may come under attack or even be destroyed. The Israelis may not notice the sound of those high-flying jets, but their subconscious antennae would notice very quickly if the sound weren't there. No one doubts (least of all the Arab nations round about) that Israelis will put aside their differences in the face of a common enemy. Much more difficult, though, in the current Middle East climate, will be finding a consensus in Israel which is prepared to break out of the mental attitude of perpetual defensiveness.

To succeed, Israel would need the kind of ruthless courage and determination that were shown by those men and women, fired by idealism, who settled the land and fought for the creation of the state – the old pioneers of Zionism.

CHAPTER TWO

The old pioneers

NEW Year's Eve is not an occasion for wild celebration in Jerusalem. For a start, the rabbis don't allow it. An hotel stands to lose its 'kosher' licence from the rabbinate if it hosts a New Year party. (The High Court and the rabbinate were in confrontation over this issue in 1990.) It is true that 1 January is not the beginning of the New Year according to the Jewish calendar, but the roots of the prohibition lie in the fact that many Israelis originate from Europe where the beginning of the year is celebrated as the feast of St Sylvestre. Therefore, the rabbinical argument goes, to mark the New Year with celebrations would amount to honouring a non-Jewish festival.

Rabbinical views aside, though, many Israelis continue to observe the New Year according to the calendar observed by most of the world outside. And in Jerusalem New Year's Eve is the occasion for one particular gathering which has become an annual reunion for some fifty or sixty Israelis. It's a get-together in the living-room of a private house in the city; it's a chance to renew old acquaintances, to reminisce and to take stock of where Israel stands today. But for the past few years it has hardly been a celebration.

Several ties bind these sixty people (fewer if the weather is bad, and in any event there is a natural decline in the numbers). One common thread is their age: grey hair and weather-beaten, toughened complexions predominate. Another is that the majority are connected, or have been, with the Labour movement in Israel; some have held senior positions in the party. And thirdly they are all Ashkenazis, and secular Jews. They are part of the old guard, the pioneers who fought for the creation of the state of Israel or who smuggled arms, money and illegal immigrants into British Mandate Palestine to enable that fight to take place. They are the

Jews of Palestine who became Israelis when the British flag was lowered from Government House for the last time; they are the Israelis who built the structures of the new state.

This annual New Year's Eve gathering is a quiet, civilized affair, befitting the company. Over recent years, though, the atmosphere has become increasingly despondent. Israel has survived; but beyond that the old-timers can see little in the way the country is going that gives them cause for celebration.

What has happened to the dream? It is a question often asked by both Israelis and foreigners, but the old pioneers take issue with the wording of the question. These grey-haired Israelis, chatting in small groups in the crowded living-room, have a look of ruggedness. They were clearly 'doers', men and women of action rather than starry-eyed dreamers. It is not what happened to the dream that concerns them, but what became of the reality which they created.

The atmosphere of those early days is not easy for young Israelis to imagine. The younger generations take for granted the existence of, for example, the Dizengoff Centre in Tel Aviv (a large indoor complex containing shops and restaurants) and the Hilton and Sheraton Hotels. Stories of the pioneering days are part of their education, but they belong in the category of history, the category of old photo-albums crammed with black-and-white snapshots of men in shorts working the land or bringing illegal immigrants ashore, of the early political leaders addressing meetings with that same outdoor, pioneer look – the open-necked shirt with rolled sleeves – which for several decades was the hallmark of Israeli politicians. Today the jacket and tie is the uniform for most politicians in Israel, as it is in Egypt and Syria as much as in Britain or the United States. But still I find, among foreigners who haven't spent time in Israel, that the image of the open-necked, no-frills Israeli politician persists. The pioneer image of Israel is one that is attractive to many outsiders and remains one that they are reluctant to drop.

Jewish leaders before and after the creation of the new state faced a number of major challenges. Hundreds of thousands of Jews from around the world poured in and had to be fed and housed, against a background of gigantic economic problems and a collapsed currency. Also urgent matters relating to security had to be addressed. The underground resistance movements had to be turned into the nation's army. Soldiers of the new army were men who had had plenty of experience of battle and guerilla warfare (or should one say 'terrorist activity'?). To what degree military means justify the ideological end is largely a matter for debate. At what point does freedom-fighter become terrorist, or terrorist become freedom-fighter? The debate continues in the same land but in a different context because of the political and nationalist aspirations of the Palestinians. Old-timers acknowledge, as one of them told me, that on occasion 'bad things were done to the Palestinians just as there were savage acts committed when the Haganah [the main Jewish underground defence organization] tried to destroy the Irgun [a more radical and extreme rival group]. But we tried to operate by the concept of "purity" of weapons. Imperfectly, but we tried to live by it.' He was contrasting the élite ideals of the army at that time with today's Israeli army whose members one can see harassing and humiliating, and at times using brutal methods against, the Arab population of East Jerusalem and the occupied West Bank and Gaza Strip. Differences in ideals and in humanitarian considerations there may have been in those early days, but the revelation of such differences will do little to dissipate the bitterness of Palestinians who remember what happened at the village of Deir Yassin (more than 200 civilians killed in a massacre following an attack by Irgun and members of the Stern Gang on the Arab village near Jerusalem in April 1948) and elsewhere. Just as the detailed exposition of the ideological motives which spurred Arab gunmen to kill nine Israeli tourists in an attack on a tourist bus in Egypt early in 1990 would do little to console the families of the victims.

History is a blunt weapon, whether it is in the hands of the Arabs or the Israelis. Having lived and worked on both sides of the Middle East conflict, I have seen it used to bludgeon every tender seedling of hope that the peoples of the region (not least the Israelis) might break out of their shells of defensiveness. Inevitably, too, the longer the wait for a breakthrough, the greater the chance that frustrations will spill over into acts of violence; and these in turn serve only to encourage those wielding the weapons of 'history'.

The army of the new Israel (henceforth known as the Israel Defence Force or IDF), having fought off the military challenge from the Arabs in the war of independence, had to secure the borders. As the government tried to attract foreign investment and develop industry, immigrants were settled in new development towns around the country or were encouraged to set up kibbutzim (economically independent collectives) or moshavim (agricultural co-operatives where farms are owned by individuals) close to the borders.

On 29 January 1949 a group of Israelis opened up and cleaned out an abandoned Nissen hut on the site of what had once been a British army base close to the sea just south of the Lebanese border. That night the founding members of Kibbutz Gesher Haziv ate their first meal together in the Nissen hut. The hut next door became the cowshed. For the members of the kibbutz, that first night and many thereafter were spent in tents pitched in the tangle of overgrown orchards. Those were difficult days. I met several people who spent that first January night in 1949 in Gesher Haziv, and neither they nor anyone who joined the community in the months that followed spoke with anything but warmth and enthusiasm about their pioneering days.

Nachman Goldwasser, one of the founders of Gesher Haziv, is now in his mid-sixties. Standing in his blue overalls, tending the salad and vegetable plots which provide food for the 500 or so people who live on the kibbutz, he talked about the early days. The site had been chosen because it was an area of rich soil, or so they had thought at the time. Later they learnt that much of the land was of poor quality. The early months were spent clearing the undergrowth, and then seeing what could be retrieved from the orchards, which had once belonged to a nearby (by that time deserted) Arab village. And not just the first months, but the first years, too, were spent clearing the stones from the fields. The saying on the kibbutz is that rocks evidently grow on the land, because every time you plough you get more. Work from morning until night characterized the early period, and until wooden huts were built (first for the children) the workers remained under canvas. Nachman Goldwasser's son was born while they were all living in tents. Despite the hardships, such as the heavy snow of the severe winter of 1950 which made the tents collapse, Goldwasser recalled these as exciting times. 'We had a new country and new people. We were in on the ground floor. And there was great idealism and a sense of euphoria at the beginning of the state.'

Hardship blending sweetly with euphoria is the common theme of memories of the early days at Gesher Haziv. Eliezer Nir, another founding member ('I arrived here straight out of the army with nothing more than a kitbag'), remembers both the shortages of food in the country and the efforts to combat malaria. Yet, 'There was a good feeling of accomplishing and building.' And Margalit Hadari (her first name before she emigrated from the United States was Marsha) insisted that she wasn't gazing at the past through rose-tinted spectacles when she talked of the first two years at the kibbutz as 'the romantic period. It was probably the loveliest little home I ever had, that little tent. Despite the austerity and shortage of food there was a "together" feeling. We had a reason for being here and were very idealistic.'

The original Nissen hut with curved corrugated-iron roof, which the members of Gesher Haziv used as their meeting- and dining-hall, is still standing, abandoned and now almost lost behind overgrown shrubs and overhanging tree branches. Sheets of corrugated iron have been nailed over the windows and doors. Much has changed at Gesher Haziv, as we shall see, and not just in the style of buildings. Much has changed with the whole kibbutz movement, not least the fact that its interested protector, the Labour party (an Israeli Labour party detached from the kibbutz movement is unimaginable), has lost the position that it enjoyed in Israel in the early 1950s.

In the current turbulent atmosphere of Israeli politics it is hard to imagine a period when one party dominated the scene in the way that Labour did in the early years of the state. Labour had controlled the Jewish Agency (which organized the immigration of Jews and the transfer of funds to Palestine) in pre-state days, and took control of government when the state was formed. An old-timer who was involved with the Labour movement remembers the early leaders as being an élite, having a strong identity and empathy with European and north American Jewry. Not surprisingly, Labour old-timers speak with nostalgia of that period. 'There was a passion, a dedication to Zionism and a shared identity with the Jewish people which are no longer to be found in Israel,' one told me. 'That generation had directly experienced what I can only call the "yiddishness" of Eastern Europe. They had the *Yiddishkeit*, the warmth, the humour. Today the humour is sour. There are jokes but no humour.' The Labour leaders then, he went on, 'were loving, if not always lovable; they were full-blooded, passionate people. Large in every way. Their infighting was passionate, their sins and their accomplishments were passionate too. It's difficult to think of a "cold" person in that group. Someone might have killed for ambition, but it wasn't ambition alone.'

An example of this informal and personal style of leadership was

Golda Meir's kitchen cabinet. When she was Prime Minister (between 1969 and 1974) key members of her cabinet were invited every Friday night to an informal meeting, literally in her kitchen. She would cook some kind of Yiddish meal for her colleagues while they discussed affairs of state. No minutes were taken; no elections were held for places around the kitchen table.

All this wasn't to suggest, though, that Labour had matters all its own way, or that the path for Labour itself was always smooth. The party had its share of scandals and intrigues, its divisions and desertions; and the political stage had as varied a group of actors on it then as today. No fewer than twenty-seven political parties registered in the 1988 general elections, the fragmentation of political groups reflecting the wide diversity of backgrounds and influence that make up Israeli society. What surprised me, though, was to learn that in the early elections to the Knesset there was a similar range of voting choices. And while the Labour left governed, its performance was monitored closely by parties on the right, the liberals and Herut (led by the former Irgun leader Menachem Begin) which acted as an opposition group in the Knesset. Disagreements between rival politicians inside one party and rivalries between opposing parties existed then as much as they do today, and with as much anger and emotion. But political observers recall that these emotionally violent exchanges both inside and outside the Knesset were conducted within certain bounds of restraint. Chaotic scenes like that witnessed during a meeting of the Central Committee of the Likud bloc in February 1990 would at one time have been unimaginable. At that meeting the Israeli public, via television, saw their Prime Minister, Yitzhak Shamir, and a senior Likud minister, Ariel Sharon, trying to shout each other down as each appealed for support from the audience, which was itself involved in its own shouting match. The meeting ended in undignified pandemonium. This was Israeli democracy at work – but Israeli democracy 1990s-style, reflecting the hot-tempered and hysterical aggressiveness that now lurks below the surface of society. For anyone present in the hall that night this seemed like an apocalyptic moment in the country's politics. But in the Middle East hysterical passions subside as quickly as they are roused. The next morning much that had been said in the anger of the moment was forgotten.

The first generations of Knesset members were selected from the top ranks of both the left and right wings of society, and they did their best to set and maintain standards. Within the chamber members never addressed one another (friend or enemy) by name alone but by the title Haver (Member of Knesset). Nowadays when tempers reach flashpoint they occasionally drop this courtesy. That pillar of the Labour Establishment and indeed of the whole political establishment, David Ben-Gurion, made the headlines in the early 1960s when in the Knesset he called Menachem Begin a clown. The shock which that utterance caused is an indication of the decorum with which political debate had been conducted for the first decade and a half of Israel's existence. And it is an indicator of how far political life has sunk in the years since: personal abuse has become the order of the day when passions are roused. Insults are inelegant, unsubtle and lacking in wit or style. In the days leading up to that meeting of the Likud central committee mentioned above, one of Mr Shamir's critics, a minister from his own party, made a cruel reference to his lack of physical height by describing him as being like a dwarf trying to interfere in a game of basketball. The number of speakers with a flare for oratory has declined, veteran Knesset correspondents say, as the calibre of candidates being put forward on party lists as potential holders of Knesset seats has also dropped.

The slide of Knesset debates, and political dialogue in general, into what one observer described as the atmosphere of a Middle Eastern bazaar has done nothing to win the respect of the public for politicians and the political system. A study based on opinion polls conducted in 1989 revealed the attitudes of the Israeli public towards the twelve major democratic institutions of the country. On the question of how much they trusted these institutions, the IDF (Israeli Defence Force) came out on top; the Knesset came fifth, after the courts system, the universities and the police; and political parties (along with the media and the trade union Histadrut movement) brought up the rear.

The work of the pioneers of the Jewish state (giving substance to the dream) was put to the test in the Arab-Israeli war of June 1967. The crushing defeat inflicted on the Arab armies in that six-day conflict seemed to put the icing on the cake. Israel had defied the odds by being created in the first place; it had further defied the odds by surviving in the face of external threats and severe economic difficulties; and now it had trounced its toughest enemies. The war also gave substance to another dream: the Arab eastern half of Jerusalem was captured from the Jordanians, giving Jews control of the remaining wall of the last Jewish temple – the Western, or Wailing, Wall. Looking through Israeli eyes, the capture of East Jerusalem was an unqualified triumph. The capture of the West Bank and Gaza Strip, on the other hand, was not universally applauded; and the continued occupation of the territories has exposed splits within society which have undermined some of the principles espoused by the old pioneers, and have even tarnished some of the euphoria associated with what the Israelis called the 're-unification' of Jerusalem.

Teddy Kollek was Mayor of Jerusalem before the 1967 War. All the triumph and all the sadness of the pioneer generation are written in the lines of fatigue on the face of this veteran campaigner, who came from Vienna to live on a kibbutz in Palestine in 1936. An old friend of Teddy Kollek remembers the excitement when the decision was taken to 'pull down the huge ugly walls dividing the city which you could see from every street. Arabs poured in here and Jews poured in there.' In the euphoria, Israeli expectations ran high, and for a time the excitement seemed to be justified. Teddy Kollek knew, though, that to keep the city together would take hard work. He made, as his personal crusade, the idea of one Jerusalem with the two communities co-existing and with equal rights for all. 'And look what's happened,' his friend continued. 'When the Palestinian uprising broke out Kollek never thought it would come to Jerusalem. But it did.' Jerusalem, the city regarded by Israel as its capital for ever, once again became divided. No wall has been rebuilt, but you can feel the psychological barrier that now keeps the two communities apart.

Teddy Kollek is one of the old-timers who attends the New Year's Eve reunion in Jerusalem. These days, his friends say, he is more depressed than anyone. 'We all feel desperate at what's going on today; he's destroyed. This city is his whole life. In this narrow space where we get together at New Year you can feel the shelter that his friends build around him.' Teddy Kollek's vision of a unified Jerusalem springs from his vision of Zionism. The occupation of the West Bank and Gaza Strip, and the justifications for their continued occupation put forward by politicians on the right, do not conform with those visions, as he explained in a newspaper article written early in 1990: 'Now more than ever I can appreciate David Ben-Gurion's clear statement, in June 1967, that while the bond of our heritage to Jerusalem would make a redivision of the city unthinkable, almost everything else should be returned quickly. Ben-

Gurion was surely a patriot, but not of today's kind. He was a realist and a humanist as well . . .' In the current political climate Teddy Kollek feels isolated.

The military triumph of Israel in 1967 marked the beginning of the end of an era. An artist, Anita Kushner, settled in Israel from the United States two years after the war. She remembers 'a different kind of Israel' from today, one marked by 'euphoria, self-confidence and optimism. One expression typified that time. Whenever you talked about anything in your life – I have a big overdraft, a problem with this, that or the other, or my leg hurts; or there is a big quarrel in the Knesset, or there's something politically amiss, it doesn't matter what – the end of the conversation, whether it was with Sephardis or Ashkenazis, at a high or low intellectual level – always the end of every conversation was: "Yihye tov", it will be good, everything will be OK. And I feel now today I almost never hear anybody say that. Almost never. Here and there a real old-timer will say: "Yihye tov."'

The desire of many sections of Israeli society to establish settlements in the newly conquered land and thus make the surrender of those territories more difficult, created divisions within Israel that set the country on the path to polarization that characterizes it today. And the optimism and euphoria that the 1967 War inspired were defused painfully by the setbacks of the 1973 conflict where an over-confident military was caught off guard. The assumption of military superiority was challenged. But Israelis did not question the moral superiority of their fighting force or the political leadership directing it until the Lebanon War of 1982.

By this time much had happened to make the old guard gloomy – not least the shock of hearing in May 1977 that Labour's monopoly of power had been ended by the party's old enemy Menachem Begin. With hindsight it is not difficult to realize that Labour's time had run out; and given the number of years in which they'd held on to power it is perhaps not surprising that they and their supporters should have been the last to realize the significance of the changes going on around them. The party had been discredited by the fiasco of the 1973 War and by a number of financial scandals. The respectability of Mr Begin and his Herut party had grown, attracting the votes of many of the Sephardi community who had felt excluded from the world of politics by the Labour élite. Israel had changed. It has been a bitter pill for the old guard to swallow, left as they are to take those seats in the grandstand allocated for the retired professionals. The performance of the new teams on the field doesn't meet much with their approval: the rules of politics have changed, leaving it a rougher game, one more suited to the Middle East than to Europe or the United States. The world outside, too, needs to understand that the rules have changed in this way.

Israeli politicians were not slow to realize that a call for a renewal of the 'pioneering spirit' (and they didn't necessarily mean the settlement of the West Bank and Gaza Strip) was a strong emotional card to play when trying to win support for a cause. I witnessed an interesting example of this in the middle of 1987 when I arrived in Israel.

The debate of the day centred on the future of the Lavi fighter jet being built by Israel Aircraft Industries at Ben Gurion airport near Tel Aviv. The Lavi (in Hebrew meaning 'lion') was extremely advanced in many of its features. It seemed to be an example, all too rare in the late '80s following the national trauma of the Lebanon War, of 'little' Israel defying the odds and proving that nothing was beyond its ability. The only problem was: the Lavi was being largely funded by the United States, and the Americans said, in as many words, that the project had become too expensive and would therefore have to be scrapped. By this time only prototype models had been produced.

On economic grounds there was no argument. But the anguished debate – long and heated it was, too – centred on the Lavi as a symbol of national pride, of the pioneering spirit. When the battle for the Lavi was lost, and the project scrapped, workers burnt tyres on the Tel Aviv to Jerusalem highway. 'This is typical of Israel today,' one commentator wrote, 'that we are killing off everything that has vision.'

Shortly after the Lavi affair, Israel suffered another humiliation which questioned one more basic assumption: the reputation of the armed forces. Near the end of November 1987 a Palestinian gunman attached himself to a powered hang-glider and flew from southern Lebanon through Israel's sophisticated border defence system into northern Galilee. The presence of an unidentified object crossing the border was noted and all northern settlements were put on alert. Despite this, the gunman landed and made his way to an army base. When he opened fire, the guard on duty ran away. The soldiers inside were watching television; they had not collected their weapons and were caught unprepared. The gunman killed six soldiers before being shot dead himself. 'The night of the hang-gliders', as it has become known, is important because it was one of the sparks which lit the flames of the Palestinian uprising in the Gaza Strip a few days later. Palestinians took the incident as evidence that Israel was not invincible in the face of a determined attack. They too took a fresh look at the reality of Israel.

It's that uprising, and the military and political response to it, that have made recent New Year's Eve gatherings for the group of old-timers in Jerusalem, in the words of one them, 'infinitely more gloomy than before because we are doing terrible things and there seems to be no way out and no way of addressing the problem.'

What the old pioneers find hard to swallow is that the fulfilled dream, the state that aspires to be 'a light unto the nations', has in so many ways become 'just another country'. Settling the land, draining the swamps and building towns and cities were the first priorities of the early pioneers. Plenty still needs to be done, but the basic pioneering work is complete. Israel is not an ordinary state by the very nature of its conception, by its composition and by the manner of its survival. But those traits hide the fact that much of what goes on in the country is ordinary, one might say refreshingly ordinary. Pick up a newspaper in Israel and you'll notice the obsession with security and with what Palestinians and other Arabs have been saying and doing. But a lot of the news these days is similar to that which you'll find in 'any country' – a feature about the problems of battered wives; a story of how the chief Rabbi of the Sephardi community was being flown to a hospital in Afula to try to persuade a Tunisian-born Israeli in her eighties to withdraw her refusal to undergo an operation to save her life; the trial of a man accused of several murders in the murky underworld of drugs and crime in the southern suburbs of Tel Aviv; tragedies on the road; a heart transplant at the Hadassah hospital. And so on.

Such talk brings little comfort for those fifty or sixty Israelis crowded into the Jerusalem living-room on New Year's Eve. But how, I asked one of them on another occasion, can you expect the idealism to be the same today when the pioneering work is largely done, when the land has been settled? I was missing the point, he replied. 'It's a question of what hasn't been done. We haven't built a caring society. It needn't necessarily have been socialist, just caring. Idealism was expressed by the settling of the land. But what we were doing was building a "warm" state for a "warm" people.' Evidence of that failure, he went on, is that Israel is an uncaring society today. 'We were tough and rude before, but now we've become a hard, aggressive nation both in terms of Jew unto Jew, and Jew unto Arab. The standards of what's acceptable have been lowered. Look how people behave. Look at those hysterical funerals every time Israelis are killed by terrorists. It's like a pagan orgasm.'

Professor Ephraim Katzir, who was President of Israel in the late 1970s, addressed the issue of relations with the Palestinians in an interview with *Hadashot* newspaper in April 1989:

> The Zionist dream was not to create a Jewish state in which Arabs are beaten up; our dream was to have a state of which the Jewish people could be proud. Many of my friends were killed in the war of independence. Was this only in order to make ourselves strong? I believe that the Jewish people and the enlightened world will not let us degenerate, and that we will get ourselves out of the present predicament . . .

In the view of several old-timers I've met, many of the reasons for 'the present predicament' lie in the failure of the leadership. 'I think we've about come to deserve the leadership we've long had. A few years ago we didn't,' one commented. Certainly, politicians neglect the social services, like education and health. This attitude is accompanied by what I have heard described as 'an endemic lack of interest on the part of individuals on all these issues'.

Personal ambition and materialism, it seems, increasingly motivate the public and politicians alike. Israel is not a rich country, indeed its economy is in serious difficulties. Yet the demand for consumer goods, as anywhere else, has blossomed, to the point of obsession. Anita Kushner, returning to Israel in 1984 after a two-year absence, was struck by the change. 'People were driving new cars; all of a sudden Israelis had Volvos, Mercedes. I couldn't believe my eyes. And these big fancy houses. I'd liked the idea that I was living in a socialist country, and suddenly it looked like the capitalism of the States all over again.' Orielle Berry, who is in her mid-thirties and came from South Africa, says there's a 'fanaticism for buying new things all the time. Begin gave the Sephardis everything and that's where the rot set in and people started living on the "never-never". It annoys me when I go to my relatives and all they talk about is where you can buy the latest this, that and the other. I could buy things cheaply when I arrived because of certain rights given to new immigrants, but I didn't buy the biggest and most expensive. "Why do you buy such a small fridge when you have the new immigrant's rights?" And I said: "I don't need it, I don't want it." Almost like children who've never been given permission, and all of a sudden they have been given the facilities and have to go out and do it in the biggest way they can.'

The world of the kibbutz and moshav has not escaped this materialism, though the introduction of consumer luxuries was slow; resistance to change was frequently stubborn. Kibbutzniks at Gesher Haziv told me of the heated arguments for and against the electric kettle and every other gadget. If individuals were allowed kettles in their rooms, the argument ran, then people wouldn't rely so much on the communal facilities and the communal spirit would suffer. The same arguments were put forward by those who opposed the installation of telephones, fridges and televisions in private rooms. There was also the argument of money: if one family wanted a particular luxury it could be allowed only if the kibbutz could afford to provide the same for everyone else. The restriction on televisions was one of the last ones to fall. Now the kibbutz provides a black-and-white set for all members, and individuals are allowed to buy colour ones if they want. Television aerials have appeared on most accommodation buildings.

The lines are being drawn in Gesher Haziv for the next assault on the traditional spartan life-style: some members want to be allowed to have their own cars. At present the kibbutz has a pool of about twenty cars which are used on kibbutz business or can be booked out by members.

Zvi Baer is one member totally opposed to the introduction of cars. Looking back to the early '50s when he arrived in Israel, he laments the fact that 'We've become much more materialistic.' He says the change began in 1958. The austerity years following the setting-up of the state were over and people were beginning to acquire money. 'Things were going well so we started thinking about ourselves. Up to then we'd never had the time. So the arguments started about whether we should be allowed a little fridge in our houses. There were arguments, committee meetings and a general assembly discussion. There was opposition, but in the end the kibbutz undertook to buy some. That meant we were already up one small notch. Then came fancy phonographs, and so on.' On the question of cars, though, Zvi Baer thinks that 'the kibbutz should put its foot down.' For the kibbutz to provide a car for each family would be financially crippling.

Gesher Haziv is not flush with money, to put it mildly. The kibbutz began the 1990s in debt to the tune of 15 million US dollars, with no prospect of being able to pay that off. The whole kibbutz movement is in severe financial difficulties, which have forced kibbutzim to look for sources of income other than agriculture and the land. A few yards from the original old Nissen hut in Gesher Haziv stands a giant hangar of a building that would look more at home in an industrial zone than a kibbutz. Walk inside and you could forget at once that you were in a rural area of northern Israel. A growl of heavy machines greets you. Men in blue overalls are supervising the production machinery and monitoring electronic screens. A giant yellow crane is slowly being moved along overhead rails. Sacks full of moulded black pipes and other components are evidence that this is a plastics factory which makes a host of items including the parts for babies' high-chairs that are seen throughout Israel. In the packing-room at the far end of the hangar piles of sun-loungers are being arranged, ready for export to Italy.

Not five minutes' walk from the plastics factory is a smaller workshop where I met another of the founder-members of the kibbutz. Like his colleagues he'd spent those early pioneering days clearing the orchards and digging the stony soil. Today Ishai Harari is in his sixties and his job is working on a production line making briefcases. A lot has changed since the early days, he says; the Zionist pioneering spirit 'doesn't exist in the same way. The land has been settled. The challenges aren't the same any more.'

The fact is that the kibbutz and moshav movements are paying the price for the huge investments that they made in the 1970s, during the days of high inflation in Israel when money was flowing freely. Now, with the bubble burst, the sheltered world of the kibbutz is discovering that Israel outside has changed. And modern Israel has little patience with and little sympathy for those old-timers and inheritors of the pioneer spirit who rolled up their sleeves, worked the land and by doing so helped both to establish a Jewish security presence close to the borders and to give expression to the Zionist work ethic. Like others of the old pioneers in Israel, kibbutzniks say the major change came in 1977 when Labour lost power for the first time. Menachem Begin was merciless in his scorn for what he regarded as the privileged élite 'with their swimming-pools' – as if it were a crime for a community of several hundred people to provide for themselves a facility for bathing. Since then, I was told, there's nothing that the kibbutz movement has been able to do to eradicate the smears and counter the growing bias within a rightward-shifting population against one of the best-known institutions in Israel.

Looks are very deceptive. When you drive through the security fence into Gesher Haziv you arrive in a world that seems neat and ordered – well-kept flowerbeds and lawns, buildings showing none of the down-at-heel look which you find in many of the streets in the nearby coastal town of Nahariya. There is a kibbutz guest-house with a smart lobby, gift shop, and international credit-card stickers on the glass doors, which caters for passing tourists. Nothing on the face of it indicates that times are hard. Indeed the air of affluence is detrimental to the efforts of the kibbutz movement to convince the largely sceptical Israeli public that kibbutzim need urgent financial help. When they drive past one in a bus it looks like an oasis of green calm and affluence. The comfortable appearance masks the reality. It is not uncommon these days for kibbutz members to go to their treasurer to withdraw their allocated spending money, only to be told: today the coffers are empty.

'In the old days we had a very pioneering atmosphere,' Geula Shoham told me in Gesher Haziv. 'We worked hard and were devoted. Now the whole kibbutz movement is in crisis financially and ideologically. The whole country has changed. Before, it was socialist, the Labour party was ruling. Now it's the other way round. Now the people are against the aspirations of the kibbutz movement. They hate the Labour party, they hate us. One of the biggest problems is attracting the younger generation. In fact, they're gradually leaving. The whole dream has shattered. The whole atmosphere of Israel has changed.'

In the kibbutz dining-hall there were plenty of young faces, and the chatter was lively. Lunch that day consisted of broccoli soup, with a choice of fish or meat-loaf, and a large variety of salads. Wholesome fare. Shaul Ben David is a grandfather; his daughter and baby grand-daughter live on the kibbutz. Shaul's journey to Israel began in Burma. During the Second World War, when the Japanese invaded Burma, his family and the rest of the small Jewish community moved to India. Shaul joined the Zionist Youth movement there; the fact that he was a refugee, he says, influenced his desire to find a homeland, and in 1949 he stepped off a charter plane carrying his kitbag containing 'gumboots, a blanket and little else'. Despite the major changes that have occurred, Shaul Ben

David is totally committed to the ideals of the kibbutz movement. As for the younger generation, he admits that the influence of life outside is strong ('it's not easy being on an oasis, with life going on outside'), especially given the prevailing mood of materialism in Israel as a whole and the financial crisis in the kibbutz movement.

Zvi Baer's son was on leave of absence from Gesher Haziv when I was there. Like all parents Baer hopes that the younger generation will eventually settle back after they finish their army duty and return from a spell of travel overseas, which for many young Israelis is the next step after the army. But he too is realistic about the pressures, not least the economic ones, which pull the youth away. When founders of Gesher Haziv, like Zvi Baer, established the kibbutz they were prepared to ignore the hardships because they had a clear ideological mission to settle the land close to the border. But it's not easy, he says, to instil that same spirit in the younger generation, who don't look at kibbutz life in the same way. In fact, 'they are quite materialistic. Some still want to take part in collective life, some don't. We're quite lucky, with our youth it's about half and half.'

Trying to recreate the spirit of a departed era is a battle that probably will be lost. Equally, though, to write the obituary of the kibbutz would be wrong. Kibbutzniks at Gesher Haziv point to the numbers within their own community which remain about constant, despite the comings and goings. While young people out of the army may prefer to go abroad there is continual interest from people in their mid-twenties – young couples who want to escape from the urban rat-race and find physical and emotional security for their children. Shortly before I visited Gesher Haziv the kibbutz had celebrated its forty-first birthday. The atmosphere at the celebration, I was told, was not clouded by the fact that the kibbutz was fifteen million dollars in the red. (Because of the fluctuating value of the shekel all business dealings are conducted in dollars.) Economic pressures are not felt so acutely by individuals in the way that they would be in society outside. Come what may, the basic necessities of life are provided for; and the community as a whole pulls together to help those in need.

The pressures on families living on moshavim are similar to those living on kibbutzim: how to survive in the face of economic difficulties and changes in the outlook of the younger generation. Sometimes these pressures lead to serious crises within individual communities. Ramot

Naftali is perched on a rocky ridge of hills right up against the Lebanese border; at night it is not uncommon to hear the sound of shelling and gunfire coming from Lebanon and to see the night sky lit by flares. The community of eight families at Ramot Naftali is split half-and-half over the question of what path the moshav should follow to try to cope with its financial difficulties. One group decided that they would no longer be part of the central distribution system, but would go it alone. The other group favoured carrying on with the original centralized system. The split caused immeasurable damage to the community; one half simply stopped communicating with the other.

For Esther and Avram Adler, who are in the their forties with four children, the division in the community was just the latest in a string of difficulties. Because of the shortage of money on the moshav, both Esther and Avram have second jobs outside. Esther is a secretary at the regional office of the local moshav movement; Avram is a cold-storage technician. According to the rules of movement the eldest child has the right to a farm of his own, and with twenty more farms available in Ramot Naftali, paid for by the Jewish Agency, the prospects for the Adlers' twenty-one-year-old son look reasonable. But with no money available to expand the family farm, and with a limit to the amount of available land (and therefore potential income), the Adlers are not so optimistic about the younger children being able to stay. Indeed, Esther says she doesn't want her sons to pin their future on Ramot Naftali. 'I advise them to go to the big world and look after themselves, be independent, learn a job, a profession, study and not depend on agriculture.' The Adlers conclude with evident sadness that 'times are changing. What was good forty years ago when our parents came here isn't good any more. The value of the work is not as high as it was before. People are looking for an easier life. It's as if it's a shame to be seen in working clothes.'

What has happened to the image that the outside world still has of Israel, with the dedicated Zionist out in the field with his sleeves rolled up working the land?

Avram Adler says: 'You see Arabs doing it instead. Jews want to be managers. Hard work doesn't become them any more.'

The question of Israel's relationship with the Arabs in the Occupied Territories is one that concerns the inhabitants of kibbutzim and moshavim whom I met as much as the financial difficulties and the evaporation of Zionist idealism. I found very considerable anger and resentment among them at the way that Jewish settlements in the Occupied Territories appeared to receive preferential treatment in the provision of social services and other amenities; and fear that there could be civil warfare if a day arrived (and most people I met in these communities hoped it would) when Israel surrendered at least part of the Occupied Territories in exchange for peace.

But among the old pioneers and their offspring I found again and again, to a greater or lesser extent, the same doubts and same despair: the distrust of politicians; the distrust of internationally guaranteed arrangements for Israel's security; the basic distrust of Arabs. But above all I found a lack of faith in anything positive being achieved in the search for peace. Margalit Hadari at Gesher Haziv expressed her feelings in the following way: 'My children and my husband support Peace Now. But I'm so confused I don't know what to think, and that disturbs me greatly . . . I don't know what the answers are. Maybe one tries to turn the other way when things become too complex, you feel you don't have the solutions, so you'd rather not get sick thinking about it. Fatalism, that's the word, perhaps. I think that I have an ostrich feeling. I'd just rather not even talk about the problem or think about it, and that frightens me.'

Adopting the posture of an ostrich is hardly something that would have occurred to Israelis during the pioneering days. Then, the issues were clear, or so it seems on looking back. The problems were big, but the big-hearted pioneers, fed on a nutritious diet of idealism, were more than equal to the challenges. It was a romantic, heroic story which Israel and much of the world outside the Middle East loved to hear. Israelis enjoyed playing their role, and the thought that it would change never crossed their minds. However, changes did creep up on society, with the loss of confidence brought on by the 1973 Middle East War, the disastrous war in Lebanon, and the Palestinian uprising in the occupied West Bank and Gaza Strip. In the process, Israel's image began to change. 'This time,' Eleanora Lev, news editor of the *Maariv* newspaper commented in 1988, 'we're not on the side of the red-headed David, that heroic scamp, God's darling, the crowd-pleasing favourite. This time we're that fool Goliath, weighed down by our armour, and you know how the story ends. After so many years of unclouded self-love, how painful it is to wake up and discover this wound, this coarse and ugly nakedness.'

It is not easy for older Israelis and supporters of Israel to come to terms with the changes that have been taking place. Eleanora Lev says it's in part the result of a 'modification of conduct'. (Self-deception might have been a truer definition.) The romance faded, but Israelis and outsiders alike were reluctant to admit it. 'At a certain point,' she says, 'we gave up hitchhiking and sleeping under the stars, except in large groups and under guard; but we continued to think of ourselves in a small, friendly, and safe country.' And, in attitudes to the Occupied Territories, 'we made our peace with the daily abominations of discrimination and injustice, and we benefited from cheap labour, tax benefits and extra privileges based on devious and labyrinthine laws. But we continued to believe, wanted to believe, in the old slogans of an egalitarian society and, even, of a chosen people.'

A century ago Theodor Herzl set out a vision, a dream of modern Zionism. Sidra Ezrahi, a lecturer at the Hebrew University in Jerusalem, writing in *Tikkun* magazine in 1988, suggested that 'one hundred years later, it is not the dream itself, but dreaminess that has survived the Jewish revolution. Maybe our somnambulism is stronger than our desire for awakening.'

There are days in Israel when you feel you are walking in a dream, when the wind picks up sand from the surrounding deserts and covers the country and the surrounding Arab states in a yellowy white mist. Even in Jerusalem, 2,500 feet above both sea and desert, the normally clear, sharp air turns ghostly white and the pale stonework of the city is swallowed up. Everyday sights and sounds lose, suddenly, the comfort of familiarity. This is Jerusalem, this is Israel in a new light – not the Israel of the picture postcard or tourist brochure. It is a shadowy, shifty Israel, without clearly defined shapes, with the air so full of sand that it stings your eyes and crunches between your teeth. This is not the image that conforms to the conventional vision, so it is not what the Israelis want to show the world and it's not what the world has come to expect.

A cacophony of accents – Middle Eastern, European, South American – can be heard in the strident voices of modern-day Israel. The cacophony drowns the quiet chatter of old-timers getting together in Jerusalem to mark the passing of another year; and confuses, in my experience, many of those outside Israel who would prefer to hear the measured and reassuring tones of a single voice.

CHAPTER THREE

Israel in English

OREIGN newspaper reports attached flattering epithets to his name:
'Israel's senior elder statesman' was one, 'Israel's foremost apostle
for peace and moderation' was another. A London paper wrote
that after forty years as 'a powerful and eloquent spokesman for Israel' he
had been ousted from Israeli politics. The abrupt removal of Abba Eban
from the Labour party's list of potential Knesset members in advance of
the November 1988 general election was a surprise. In newspaper terms: a
shock. Normally the manoeuvrings within the Israeli political system
would attract, at best, scant interest from abroad. The case of Abba Eban
was an exception.

Abba Eban was every liberal-minded foreigner's favourite Israeli
precisely because he was an advocate of peace and moderation, a man of
calm reason; a dedicated Israeli, but a critic of stubborn attitudes and
extremist policies.

Abba Eban had the manner of a distinguished politician from the West
and performed like a distinguished academic as he charmed audiences
with erudite and witty speeches delivered in rich Cambridge English. He
was a man with whom a Western audience could identify. When so many
Israeli politicians appeared to be shackled by the Jewish persecutions of
the past or blinded by horrifying visions of the future, Abba Eban seemed
to talk sense – as, for example, when he addressed an audience in New
York in December 1988 and ridiculed the perceived threat to Israel from
the PLO. Is the PLO going to destroy Israel, he asked, given that the
Jewish state can mobilize an army of half a million people and is equipped
with hundreds of tanks and sophisticated aircraft? Especially given that
the Palestinian armed force is made up of little more than 17,000 men
with no tank or air support? One might as well say, he went on, that

Luxembourg could destroy the Soviet Union. 'You could get all the PLO people into the Detroit conference centre and still have three other conferences there without any of them having any contact with each other.'

Abba Eban then turned his attack on to the prophets of doom in Israel's right-wing political establishment and what he called their 'apocalyptic rhetoric'. Seeing the new generation of Likud leaders like Benjamin Netanyahu, he went on: 'In such an ecstasy of alarm I imagine that the Babylonian King Nebuchadnezzar was at the gates of Jerusalem.'

How could the Labour party remove so unceremoniously such a brilliant spokesman for Israel? The question was posed in more than a few world capitals. Abba Eban himself, when asked about his dismissal, told the London *Daily Telegraph* that he'd paid the price for non-conformity because he'd been critical of policies in the Occupied Territories and of the continuation of the occupation. Furthermore, he had no hesitation in adding that in his view the Labour party had made a mistake in ousting him and would pay for it: 'It was not an intelligent thing to do if you assume that the object of elections is to win votes.'

Abba Eban, deliberately or not, was avoiding the real issue in that interview and others that he gave at the time. Labour dropped him because the two top leaders in the party, Shimon Peres and Yitzhak Rabin, had fallen out with him on personal grounds. Abba Eban had admirers within Labour, but they fell short of campaigning on his behalf. And Abba Eban's removal came at a time when the party was reassessing the age and background of those on the list of potential Knesset members. Labour had woken up at the eleventh hour to the fact that the party was no longer in step with a large proportion of the electorate, most notably those with Sephardi roots. The image of Labour was outdated; some of its leading figures, like Mr Eban, were clearly not at home in the earthy world of Middle Eastern politics where use of grammatical Hebrew and stylish English is not a vote-catcher.

Was it just a case of Abba Eban's day having passed, as must happen to every politician and statesman? I discussed the matter with an Israeli old-timer from the Labour party. To my surprise he said bluntly that Abba Eban had never been 'a true Israeli'; the country had never taken him to its heart in the way that he had won hearts abroad. The old-timer recalled that when Mr Eban was Foreign Minister in the Ben-Gurion government, visitors to Israel used to assume that he would become the next Prime

Minister. They saw his 'towering intellectual stature' and his image as world statesman; they didn't see him as a man who 'could not be acceptable to the Israeli electorate. He was too impenetrable a person.' There was an occasion, the old-timer went on, which showed how Eban was viewed by the Israeli public. It was after the death of a former Mayor of Jerusalem, Gershon Agron, when a huge crowd had gathered to pay their last respects. Golda Meir arrived. The crowd immediately opened up a passage for her. A step or two behind Golda Meir came Abba Eban. But the crowd closed ranks again the instant that Golda Meir had passed by, and eventually she had to turn back and ask the crowd to let him through, saying: 'He's with me!' In short, the old-timer concluded, Abba Eban may have been the best Foreign Minister and the best ambassador, and so on, but he could never have been in Golda Meir's 'kitchen cabinet', even though he stood before the world as Israel's representative from the very first day.

That last remark is a telling one and begs the broader question of whether the voices heard most frequently and the views absorbed most easily abroad are representative of the real Israel. Because in the case of Abba Eban, even leaders of his own Labour party had felt many years before his eventual dismissal that he was something of an outsider. In my view, the danger of the world at large being drawn to voices from Israel because they are alluring and accessible is a serious one. The effect is to give a distorted view of the country, even though it may be one that outsiders want to hear.

There is no doubt that the ability to communicate lucidly in English is a great advantage for any one trying to carry the Israeli flag abroad. If one looks at the two major figures on the Israeli political stage in the late 1980s and early '90s, Yitzhak Shamir of Likud and Shimon Peres of Labour, the difference in their images abroad was considerable. Mr Peres has an urbane manner, and his command of English is such that he can berate, charm or tease his audience with equal aplomb. Mr Shamir's manner, on the other hand, is awkward in public gatherings, and his command of English does not allow him much in the way of emotional cadences. An even more striking example is that of the Moroccan-born Likud minister David Levy. His hopes for taking over one day as Prime Minister are handicapped by the fact that he does not speak English. In June 1990 David Levy was made Foreign Minister: but he was appointed by a strong Prime Minister (Yitzhak Shamir) who was always going to take key foreign policy decisions himself. There are differences in policy, of course, between Likud and Labour; and it might be argued that because of this Mr Peres has a natural advantage over Mr Shamir in trying to win support in most Western countries. If their roles were reversed, though, I believe that the views and attitudes of the right wing in Israel would be much better understood abroad.

If Abba Eban is even now a favourite spokesman of Israeli politics, Amos Oz (several of whose books have been translated into English and are easily available) must carry Israel's literary banner. Aloma Halter wrote in the Israeli arts magazine *Ariel*:

> The outside world, including the kindly disposed Diaspora, looking at Israel through the black and white bars of the international press, through contradictory and confusing myths, finds it convenient that there be something quintessential to represent Israel and someone who can convey what it is all about. Someone disinterested, yet involved, representative yet individual; a poet, a novelist. For it is easier to listen to a few, clear voices than to hear a polyphonous clamour.

Exactly so. It works the other way, too:

> If it is convenient for the outside world to have Israel demystified, for its own benefit, it is also deeply satisfying for Israelis to feel that they have a voice, a popular spokesman; that this nation, surrounded by belligerence, has a window to the world, a way of explaining, at least, if not of justifying itself.

Amos Oz's books, some centred on traditional life on a kibbutz, are popular in Israel, and are studied in schools and colleges. But Amos Oz the man is by no means popular for his political views: he stands somewhere to the left of centre and is a frequent speaker at rallies of Peace Now, a protest group which advocates immediate and direct dialogue with the Palestinians. I asked a prominent figure in the Israeli right wing if he was happy that Amos Oz was the chief literary spokesman for Israel. 'Not at all,' was his instant reply. 'At one time, with his kibbutz writings he represented the mainstream of sensitive Israeli thinking. These days he's a spokesman for the left, he just doesn't communicate with the majority of Israeli thinking. I regret losing him; but today I reckon he speaks for no more than ten per cent of Jewish Israelis.'

Figures like that are clearly the result of impressions rather than research. But I have a nagging feeling that while Amos Oz in his writings and speech-making is as sincere as Abba Eban was in his career as a politician and diplomat, the same underlying danger exists: that the clear, intelligible and (to many Western readers) reasonable voice of Amos Oz will be taken as that of the majority. Indeed, is he really, as Aloma Halter writes, 'a voice, a popular spokesman'? That is very much open to question, I would say. Take, for example, a review in the *Jerusalem Post* of Oz's book *The Slopes of Lebanon*:

> The first 80 pages do little more than demonstrate that Oz had no hesitation in condemning the invasion of Lebanon, even as the fighting was still going on; reprinting these articles now in English comes off largely as an exercise in credential-waving before liberal anglophones. The subsequent items on the evils of Gush Emunim ['Bloc of the Faithful' – the group leading the drive to settle the Occupied Territories] and of the Likud government are similarly more notable for the moral outrage of a man who feels 'like an exile in my own land' than for their eloquence or force of argument.

The right wing in Israel still does not play a leading role in cultural life ('Left-wing groups are just much better organized than we are,' was one explanation I heard); and so while its voice within society may be growing, this growth will not necessarily be reflected in voices heard outside. For many decades one of the leading platforms on which Israel's views were displayed, the English-language *Jerusalem Post* newspaper, was in the hands of the centre-left in Israel. It closely reflected the views of the Labour movement. The *Post* has an importance which is out of all proportion to the size of its readership (about 50,000). Those readers include foreign diplomats and correspondents who draw freely on the well of news reports and opinions contained in its pages as they prepare their own assessments of what is going on in Israel. More important still is the weekly edition of the *Post* which is sold to some 75,000 subscribers abroad. For them, this publication is the prime source of news about Israel. For those who retain fondly the notion that Israel is an extension of Chicago or Golders Green there is plenty to feed the illusion, with columns on gardening, consumer affairs, and so on. The *Jerusalem Post* emerged out of the *Palestine Post* of the British Mandate days. Decades later the paper still sometimes has the rather pretentious pomposity of a British provincial weekly. 'Laurence Olivier bestrode the narrow world of stage and film like a Colossus,' readers were told one Friday. The great actor played 'myriad roles'. Some, the television writer continued, were vulgar and crude, and these, 'to my mind marred his performances of very sophisticated and multi-faceted parts . . . I hope that Israel Television or Channel Two or the Educational Programme will have the wit to give us a solid week of Olivier's TV films, one a night, as is done on similar occasions overseas.' And what local paper would be complete without stores like: 'Tel Aviv passes tough legislation in battle against dirty dogs. Taking your dog for a walk in the city will soon require a shovel and bag . . .;' or 'Tarts reported trekking back to central Tel Aviv'?

Aside from items about pets and ladies of the night, the *Post* also spoke out against many of the actions by the Israeli army in the Occupied Territories. In 1989 this drew an accusation from the Likud Prime Minister, Mr Shamir, that the paper was undermining Israel's standing abroad. The subsequent row led to the resignation of the editor. By this stage, though, the *Post* had changed hands. It had been bought by a right-wing Canadian newspaper group which also owned the London *Daily Telegraph* and *Spectator*. The group in turn appointed a right-wing reserve colonel as publisher of the *Jerusalem Post*. His presence prompted the resignation of around thirty editorial staff who then tried and failed to secure financial backing for a new 'liberal' paper. At the same time plans for a new weekly news magazine in English were well advanced. Both the numbers of readers and the advertising revenue for English publications are limited, but the enthusiasm to start such projects is an indicator of the perceived potential of projecting Israel's image abroad. Such publications could have commercial prospects among Jewish and other readers overseas; and some sponsors could see them as weapons for possible use in the information struggle. The message seems to be that while the liberal Establishment in Israel has enjoyed something of a monopoly over most of the years that the state has been in existence, the right is just beginning to fight back.

As well as satisfying a need overseas, the English-language press meets a considerable demand inside Israel. There is, in fact, a monthly magazine with the unambiguous title, *In English*. Here you can read, among the reports of political developments in Israel, items that interest those

Israelis who have not severed cultural links with their old country. *In English* will tell you, for example, about the activities of the Arsenal supporters' club in Israel. The editor of the magazine is Dov Sydney, a quietly spoken American immigrant who is a dentist by profession. In his modern office above a shopping centre in Ra'anana, a middle-class township close to Tel Aviv, he spoke about the need for *In English*: 'People can't feel at home in a country unless they're reading the press comfortably. The press is your connection with the world. No matter how many years you're in the country and have read Hebrew and feel fluent, the language you feel most comfortable with is the one you were born with. People who've made aliyah [emigrated to Israel] are aware they're missing much. Our function is to bring all the information that everyone else in Israel is hearing, plus information of particular interest to the English-speaking community like football and advertising.'

That attachment to English culture can extend a long way. Minna Givton arrived in Palestine from Britain in 1946. She lives in a small cottage in the Jerusalem suburb of Beit Hakerem, and is president of the Israeli Horticultural Society, a role which keeps her in touch with similar organizations in Britain. 'Of course I feel Israeli,' she said as she sat among her heavy and dark furniture with dark brocade curtains dividing the room, 'but I've never severed my emotional links with Britain. My life there was very happy. I'm a great protagonist of British values and culture.' Minna Givton was brought up speaking English but now switches with Hebrew according to the subject. 'For instance, humour and light anecdotes demand English.'

There's nothing heavy or old-world about the furnishings in the spacious white-washed villas in Ra'anana. Here, and in corners of nearby Herzliya and Tel Aviv itself, you can find pockets of Britain ('nice little homes from home,' is how one recent British immigrant described them) where only minimal concessions have been made to Israeli life. Terry Morris had been in Israel with his family for six years when I met him in his large open-plan living-room in Ra'anana. He had left his home in Manchester and come to Israel 'for Zionistic reasons'. The upheaval had not been entirely smooth. 'We didn't expect it to be easy, but we didn't realize what the problems were going to be.' Did the family experience problems assimilating into Israeli life? 'I have a feeling that we haven't assimilated in any way. Most of our friends are English-speaking. Our social life is virtually entirely English-speaking. Our attitudes haven't changed greatly since the day we came. And as such I don't think we can in any way be classified under the category of Israelis. We live in Israel and we're part of the country and we want to be part of the country. But I don't think that we are Israelis. As the generations go along, obviously our children and grandchildren will become Israelis.'

There are not many Hebrew volumes to be seen on the bookshelves in Ra'anana. Cultural life outside the home, too, is likely to centre on English-speaking clubs and associations, or perhaps on the Sharon Players or one of the five other amateur English-speaking drama groups in Israel. Here, as in provincial Britain, productions of comedies, uncomplicated and uncontroversial dramas, or Gilbert and Sullivan are the favourites.

Terry Morris accepts that the community in Ra'anana is kept apart from many of the problems that Israel faces, and that the cosmopolitan atmosphere there allows the family to keep its 'Englishness'. Comparing life in Israel with that in England, he says that children in Israel have 'a much less restricted life. They are freer in many respects. They are also freer to be failures. A Jew in England is part of a minority. Therefore there are lots of pressures on Jews and Jewish children there to be successful.' As for the kind of place Israel is today, with a brain drain among young academics, with the growth of the political right and the increasing influence of attitudes adopted from the Sephardi community, Terry Morris and others of similar background are not happy. 'I don't believe that politically the way things are going is the way I'd like; the powers-that-be are not doing the things I want them to do. Socially and politically the country seems to be polarizing. Living in Britain I had no right and no ability to do anything about it, so I thought I'd come to Israel and sort everything out. But of course that idea fell very early on, within about three weeks of arriving here.' Terry Morris laughed as he said this. 'But I still maintain that I have no right to live in England and to say what should happen in Israel. If I live here and take Israeli citizenship, then I have a right to speak.'

Tony Franklin came to Israel from London in 1974 when the country was in a state of shock and depression after the Middle East War of the previous year. While the process of becoming absorbed in Israel was a gradual one for him and his wife, they saw their children growing up as native-born Israelis. He too says that children enjoy the kind of freedom they wouldn't get in Britain, for they're living in a young country that is without many of the restraints you find in an older one. 'The whole attitude towards the Establishment and sacred cows doesn't exist. One of the national sports, I think, is knocking down any sign of Establishment. That's true of the kids, too. One of the negative things here is the disrespect and lack of discipline.' And a lack of idealism. Tony Franklin lived on a kibbutz for a time when he first came to Israel. 'Unfortunately there's been a failure of education to perpetuate the Zionist ideology, the attachment to the country, the land. The kids are growing up in a more materialistic society, and it rubs off on them.'

But anglophiles in Israel agree with the mass of the population in their low regard for the political system. Dov Sydney, editor of *In English*, laughed when I asked him about the extent of his faith in the political process. 'I haven't figured out what the political process is, so I haven't figured out if I have faith in it, as a matter of fact. I'm not used to it. I'm used to a real democracy [in the United States] . . One concern is that we're starting to have people coming into political power who have no historical background to the development of the country. In my mind there was always a sense of security having Jewish people in major positions who'd fought against the British or fought for independence. Maybe they were lacking slightly in political "savvy" but they had an historical perspective. But peope are not like that today, and their immaturity shows. The Israeli governmental system is fairly rudimentary. It's got a long, long way to go.'

Blind faith, is how Terry Morris sums up his attitude to the political process. 'I suppose I've developed the Israeli attitude of fatalism: one day it's got to come right, it can't carry on like this. If I didn't have this attitude I would find it very hard to continue to live here, because the situation at the moment doesn't look terribly promising.'

English-speaking Israelis agree on another thing: that the world outside has an image of Israel that is both hostile and distorted. One summer's evening I was the guest at a dinner-party in Tel Aviv given by a British immigrant couple. I was the only journalist present. The evening air was warm and we sat on the terrace for drinks and dinner. For an hour or more the conversation flowed over a range of matters. I thought perhaps the impossible was going to happen. But no. After dinner the guns against the foreign press opened up. Like so many anglophiles in Israel, many of those present were avid and critical listeners to the English-language service of the BBC World Service. All believed that there was an inherent anti-Israeli bias within the Corporation. Nothing that I could say would shake this conviction. My failure with that group of Israelis and many others is matched by my failure to shake the conviction of many Arabs I've met over the years that there is an inherent pro-Zionist bias within the BBC.

The heated comments directed at me that night in Tel Aviv were of a kind with which I became familiar during my three years in Israel. On another occasion Minna Givton expressed her views on how Israel is reported: 'I see everything as a question of Arab public relations. The money they choose to devote to that, and not to their own people, is what sways the issue. They have infinite resources, so they say what they want and influence people, and that doesn't give Israel a chance. We haven't the oil with which we can theaten, we haven't the billions to influence anybody, so we stand on our case and that gets pretty much swamped.'

I can't help but smile when I hear such statements. How often in Damascus, Amman, Tripoli, or any other Arab city, have I heard outbursts that are very similar in tone. If once, then a thousand times, I have been berated by Arabs who say that the Jewish Establishment world-wide has the money and influence to control the international media, and therefore the Arabs' case never gets a chance to be heard.

Each side, Arab and Israeli, speaks with absolute conviction. Each believes that something more should be done. Terry Morris agrees with the general Israeli view that the country and what happens within it are not reported fairly by the foreign press, but he thinks the fault lies with the Israelis' poor presentation of themselves. Jewish communities abroad, he says, faced by hostile reporting of Israel, find it difficult to speak up for the Jewish state because they're not given the material.

I have noticed a strong feeling in Israel that more should be done to control the flow of information into the hands of correspondents, who – it's assumed by definition – are hostile to the state. There are calls for increased restrictions on the freedom of movement of correspondents, especially in the occupied West Bank and Gaza Strip. In a way, such sentiments are understandable; there will always be those who favour shooting the messenger for bringing bad news. What I find stranger is the very Third-World idea that somehow the state can create and disseminate 'positive' news. In one of the emerging Gulf states many years ago I was sitting in the office of the newly appointed state censor. His desk was empty of papers, only a coffee cup and a pen lay before him. 'What sort of news will you be censoring?' I asked. 'Everything except "positive" news,' he replied. Censorship exists in Israel on military and security matters, and sometimes it is extended to other matters, as happened in 1990 when all news material relating to the immigration of Jews from the Soviet Union was subject to the blue pencil. In general, though, Israel has a more liberal attitude than any other state in the region towards the activities of the press. But the trend is towards the attitude of that emerging Gulf state, and not away from it.

The naive belief that Israel will be a better understood place if positive information is handed out persists because there is a feeling that this is what the Arabs are successfully doing. A letter to *In English* took the view that Israel's poor image in the international media was directly related to 'the off-hand way that the government treats' the foreign press.

> Our Arab cousins do it much better. Why cannot we learn from them? Let us designate a hotel on the Israeli side of Jerusalem where these ladies and gentlemen could be treated like guests, encouraged to see the Israeli side of life and partake of some truly Israeli hospitality. Perhaps from this a more understanding view of Israel's security would emerge, and those newshounds would see something other than the lounge of an East Jerusalem hotel, where they are continuously supplied with everything they require plus the latest version of the PLO's update.

A similar kind of reasoning formed the basis of arguments for the introduction of a news bulletin in English on Israel television. There was a pressing need for this, it was argued, because of the strong signal reaching Israel from neighbouring Jordan. Programmes from Amman in English, including a nightly news bulletin, are watched by tens of thousands of Israelis. Unofficial listings of Jordan TV schedules are published in the Israeli newspapers. The content of the Jordan news is varied, even though a prominent section is always devoted to the activities of King Hussein and his family; but when it comes to matters relating to Israel, the tone is far from sympathetic to the Jewish state. Therefore, the supporters of an English news service in Israel say, it's essential that an alternative be provided for overseas visitors and for those within the country who don't speak Hebrew or Arabic. Opponents of the scheme say the operation is not justified by the size of the potential audience. Israel Radio broadcasts four news bulletins in English each day: to introduce another English-language programme at this stage would simply be an anachronism in a state where Hebrew is both the common and the official language. Nonsense, says Dov Sydney, editor of *In English*, that's like saying there's no call for a local station in New York broadcasting in Hebrew or any other language.

The arguments continued. But what intrigued me was the wording of the justification for the news service which came from the man appointed to set it up. It was inconceivable, he said (scarcely hiding his irritation at the countless bureaucratic delays that piled on top of the underlying arguments), that 'given the general anti-Israel bias in the foreign electronic media, no attempt was being made here to strike a balance.' The assumptions that there was a 'general anti-Israel bias' and that by the flick of a switch some miraculous 'balance' could be struck began to sound a little like the sentiments expressed by ministries of national guidance in less-than-self-confident Third-World states.

Israel attracts a huge foreign press corps. There is an interest in Israel which is disproportionate to the size of the country or its population, because of the international concern about Israel's role within the continuing Middle East conflict; and because after the collapse of Lebanon it became one of the few states left in the region where reporters could operate in relative freedom. What is less well known, even inside Israel, is that of the 350 or so accredited foreign correspondents about a third are Israeli citizens, some working exclusively for foreign news organizations, others doing so on a part-time basis while holding positions in the domestic news media. In other words, the overlap between the domestic and foreign press corps is considerable. Therefore the criticism and abuse heaped blindly on the 'foreign press' is often misdirected. Israelis working for the overseas press at times complain about, for example, the restriction of access to the Occupied Territories in terms that reflect their worries about the erosion of freedoms in a country to which they are committed. Their attitude is different from that of a correspondent on a short tour of duty who will fight restrictions but always with the knowledge that if freedoms become drastically curtailed the loss will be to Israeli society, and he will simply move elsewhere.

Not always understood, either, is the fact that most of what appears in the foreign press about Israel, no matter how controversial or critical, has already been aired within the Israeli media. Hearing these controversies or criticisms spread abroad is what seems to enrage Israelis.

Having worked as a correspondent in Israel it seems to me that the foreign press has one major shortcoming: the tendency to give only scant coverage to the activities and views of those groups which do not have easy or automatic access to the news outlets. There is a (perhaps natural) tendency for foreigners, journalists and diplomats alike to drift towards those groups or individuals within Israel which espouse views not dissimilar to their own – in other words, towards liberal-minded, 'worldly' Israelis. When ultra-orthodox religious parties surprised everyone by their success in the general election of November 1988 most foreign diplomats and journalists were forced to admit that their contacts within the religious community up to that point had been minimal. Whenever I attended diplomatic functions in Tel Aviv the Israelis present, more often than not, were academics and politicians from the liberal centre-left of society. A senior Western diplomat was heard to comment that while he knew a lot of Israelis, most seemed to be members of the Labour party. But those Israelis whom one could broadly classify as being 'accessible', by virtue of their ability to speak a foreign language or by having a good grasp of the requirements of the international press, are not necessarily truly representative of the broad mass of the generally rightwards-shifting population.

The status of English as a language and culture within Israeli society, and the nature of the British legacy from Mandate days, are a complex subject. Britain's association with the region was such a long one that the fact that there is some residual influence is hardly surprising, despite (or perhaps because of) the bitterness between the British and Jewish communities in the years leading up to the creation of the state of Israel. The subsequent relationship has not always been easy, at the official or even at the private level. My family and I were leaving a swimming-pool at an Israeli hotel one summer morning when we discovered that we'd left some items behind. When I returned, one of the staff had found the things and handed them over. An Israeli bystander had watched it all, and commented without humour: 'You have no servants to go clearing up after you any more. The days of the Mandate are over.' On another occasion the deputy mayor of Safed took pride in showing me, a British subject, that he could recite from memory the names of seven Jews from the town who were hanged by the British military authorities in Acre in 1946. (In fact, to his embarrassment, when it came to it he could remember only six, and he had to get his assistant to ring around to get the final name; perhaps bitter memories are beginning to fade after all.)

Being faced, as a Briton, by events from the past presented in accusatory tones is not a new experience for me. There have been numerous occasions in the West Bank and Gaza Strip, and throughout the Arab world, when I've been reminded of Britain's complicity in setting up the Zionist state, from the Balfour Declaration of 1917 onwards. History can, I've found, be a tiresome burden for a visitor to the region as much as it can be a weapon in the hands of the inhabitants.

The complicated nature of British-Israeli relations at the official level is well illustrated by the manner of Britain's diplomatic representation. Britain, along with most other nations, wanted to exclude Jerusalem from the state of Israel and accord it international status, as spelled out in the United Nations General Assembly resolution of December 1949. As a result the international community (with the exception of El Salvador and Costa Rica) does not recognize Jerusalem as the capital of Israel, so the British Embassy is located close to the Mediterranean shore in Tel Aviv. Jerusalem (both the Jewish west of the city and the Arab east) are the responsibility of a Consul-General, who is located in the Arab section of the city and whose area of operation covers the occupied West Bank and Gaza Strip. Both the Embassy and the Consulate-General report directly and independently of each other to London. Visiting British ministers and other dignitaries make a point of distinguishing between their time in Israel and their time in the Occupied Territories, the one being organized by the Embassy, the other by the Consulate-General. Such a deliberate challenge to Israel's annexation of East Jerusalem and to the legality of its authority in the Occupied Territories is a source of great irritation to the Israeli government. Since the start of the Palestinian uprising the British have managed to annoy the authorities even more by holding two official parties, in Jerusalem, to celebrate the Queen's birthday – one for Israeli guests, the other for Palestinians. This has prompted the Mayor of the city, Teddy Kollek, and other dignitaries to announce publicly that they are staying away from the celebrations.

In general, Israelis don't like being told how to behave by the former Mandate power. An illustration of this came during a visit by a British Foreign Office minister towards the end of the 1980s. Delegations from the two countries sat down in the Foreign Ministry in Jerusalem, which consists of huts set in a leafy compound. (The huts, built shortly after the creation of the state of Israel, are of a style inherited without adornments from the Public Works Department of the British Mandate authorities.) The British delegation were trying to convince the Israelis of the need for a more flexible approach to the search for peace in the Middle East, and in particular for a less hostile attitude to the PLO leadership which, shortly before, had announced publicly its acceptance of Israel's right to exist.

'But we live here. We have the experience of what things are really like on the ground,' one of the Israelis said, to explain the cautious attitude of his government.

'Ah yes,' came the reply, 'but we've been here so much longer than you.' Israelis find condescension of this kind irksome in the extreme.

Sometimes it is even worse. During a visit to a refugee camp in the occupied Gaza Strip a few months after the start of the Palestinian uprising a Foreign Office Minister, David Mellor, angrily upbraided an Israeli army officer in front of the television cameras, without giving the startled officer an opportunity to explain what was going on. The scene incensed the nation. The most frequent comment was that Mr Mellor had behaved like a high-handed colonial administrator. 'Has Britain forgotten', one Israeli newspaper asked, 'that the Mandate ended in 1948?'

In general, though, Israel and Britain enjoy at the official level what one senior figure in the Foreign Ministry in Jerusalem called 'very normal relations with nothing extraordinary either way'. It's generally agreed that the bitterness which existed between the Mandate power and the Jews of Palestine in the years preceding the creation of the state of Israel has been forgotten. Relations at the official level fluctuate, mainly as a result of Britain's Middle East policies which Israelis believe are coloured by a deep-rooted pro-Arab bias in the Foreign Office. Aaron Remez flew with the Royal Air Force in the last World War and was later an Israeli ambassador to Britain. He believes there's always been 'an ambivalence in British attitudes to Israel. On the moral and humane level Britain has a soft spot for Israel. But when it comes to the point, Britain caters to its "interests" in the region, in whatever way they may be interpreted at the time, such as economic considerations or relations with the Arab world.'

As a Briton working in Israel it was interesting to discover visible legacies of the Mandate days. The tradition of playing league football matches on Saturday afternoon has survived, despite the fact that the religious community (or a good percentage of it) regards such activity as a desecration of the Sabbath. Driving around the area of the Russian Compound in Jerusalem, close to the law courts, one sees the sight, which is very unusual in Israel, of men wearing dark suits, white shirts and black ties. They are lawyers; and it is not just their dress which is a reminder of the days when British judges passed sentence in Jerusalem – the whole legal system is frequently cited as Britain's most valuable legacy. Some British laws are still on the statute books and British legal precedents are frequently quoted in the courts and in the Knesset. Just as important as these actual legacies are the traditions: 'the respect for the bench and the lack of the kind of histrionics that you find in courts in the United States,' as one Israeli journalist described them.

However, that journalist is of an age and background not dissimilar to those of Abba Eban, or President Chaim Herzog. British traditions are adapting to Middle East realities in the same way that Ra'anana and other pockets of 'Britain in Israel' will gradually perish. I was outside the courts in Jerusalem one day when a prominent Palestinian, Faisal Husseini, came out after a hearing. Members of the extreme right-wing Kach movement abused and spat at him. Chaim Herzog said later that such behaviour threatened to undermine the values of the judicial process. 'This humiliating spectacle', he commented in a radio address, 'in the hallways of a court-house, which was broadcast into the homes of millions of viewers around the world, pointed to a serious problem in this area. To this we can add the embarrassing sight of prisoners, who are innocent until proven guilty, being photographed in court without mercy as if they were in a showcase, and judged by the media before their trial.'

Many immigrants arriving in Israel over the decades have come from countries where the judicial system was in the hands of the central authorities commanding little respect and showing scant fairness or compassion. Coming to terms with the Israeli system is one part of the process of settling in. Another is understanding the political system and making sense of the pressures applied by groups representing views from far right to extreme left. These groups in turn feel the influences of sections of society advocating either totally religious or totally secular lifestyles, as well as the influence of the whole Middle East environment in which Israeli democracy battles to get its voice heard.

The Israeli voices describing in English for the benefit of audiences abroad the workings of the political system have not always given an accurate picture of how the scales are tipping. In the main, it seems, the views of Israeli 'doves' have been given prominence at the expense of those of the 'hawks'.

CHAPTER FOUR

The hawks

DUSK on the Lebanese border. Looking from Metulla across the lines of security fences a village is disappearing into the darkening folds of the surrounding hills; the green tip of the pencil-thin minaret is no longer distinguishable. I try to imagine the tanks and artillery pieces and the trucks of infantry troops which crossed over here in June 1982 when Israel invaded Lebanon under the code name 'Operation Peace for Galilee', a military adventure masterminded by the arch-hawk of Israel, Ariel Sharon.

Driving up into northern Israel, the landscape prepares you for Lebanon. The sandy beaches around Tel Aviv and Haifa give way to rock-crested coves and bays which extend all the way to Beirut and beyond. The coastal plains of the Israeli south become rolling foot-hills which curl their way into the central mountain ranges of Lebanon. Walk down the tree-shaded streets of Nahariya in summer and breathe the humid air: you're in Tyre and Sidon in your imagination more than in one of the coastal cities further south. The landscape flows smoothly from south to north, but the natural flow of people and commerce has stopped. The single railway track that follows the gentle lines of the coast from Gaza northwards disappears abruptly and unambiguously into the rocks of a blocked tunnel near the caves at Rosh Hanikra. Only military traffic passes through the security gates on the road above.

At Metulla an observation position has been set up from which visitors can gaze over into Lebanon. A plaque bears a quotation from the Book of Isaiah in Hebrew, English and Arabic. 'And they shall beat their swords into ploughshares, and their spears into pruninghooks: nation shall not lift up sword against nation, neither shall they learn war any more.' Wishful thinking. (Sprigs from a nearby rosemary bush obscure the

Arabic version, and no one has felt the need to clear them away.)

As the darkness descends a car pulls up; a young soldier in uniform gets out. Without enthusiasm and without expression he walks towards the dull complex of military buildings. He is watched by a young couple sitting on a step. The man is in uniform and his stubby Uzi sub-machine gun rests on his lap. His girl, wearing T-shirt and jeans, has her arm through his. They are silent. Another stint of military duty for two young Israeli men is about to begin. As I drive away from the Lebanese border again I am thinking of swords being beaten into ploughshares throughout the Middle East, of Uzis, Migs and Kfirs being converted into tractors and ploughs. But it's a fantasy beyond even imagination, given the hawkish attitudes in Israel and the surrounding states, given the proliferation of long-range missiles, chemical weapons and nuclear bombs. ('Israel will not be the first to introduce nuclear weapons into the region.' That is the official screen – and a rather thin screen it is – that Israeli officials are required to erect around their own country's nuclear capability. Officials can barely suppress a smirk as they mouth it.)

The anarchy in Lebanon over recent years has allowed that disaster of a country to become a breeding-ground for groups and organizations hostile to Israel. It was in pursuit of one of those organizations, the PLO, that Operation Peace for Galilee was launched in June 1982 to destroy the organization's infrastructure and drive out its members. Or at least that was the justification given at the time, before Mr Sharon's real intentions – of installing a pro-Israel President in Lebanon – were known. That particular operation turned into a full-scale invasion. Before and since, the Israeli armed forces have made scores of air-strikes and occasional land attacks on targets in Lebanon. Bases of Shiite Lebanese and Palestinian groups have been struck most frequently. When the bulk of the Israeli forces withdrew from Lebanon in 1985 a security zone was set up along the border as a buffer, with the aim of stopping would-be attackers before they reached Israel.

Lebanon is also used by Israel as a dumping-ground for unwanted Palestinian Arabs. Individuals expelled by the military authorities in the occupied West Bank and Gaza Strip are taken by helicopter and deposited, with fifty US dollars to help them on their way, on the northern edge of the security zone in southern Lebanon. In 1947 and 1948, when the state of Israel was coming into existence, tens of thousands of Palestinians headed for this same Lebanese border. Some had been forced out of their towns and villages, some had fled through fear. Others left the area with the intention of returning once the picture had become clearer and calm had returned. The 20,000 or so Palestinians from the town of Safed in northern Galilee were among those who had no choice in the matter.

Today there are no Arabs in Safed. I have this on the authority of the senior deputy mayor of the town, Shimon Koubi. And if he has his way, Arabs will never return there.

I visited Shimon Koubi in his office on the fifth floor of the municipality building. I was taken there by his sister. Our arrival was a scene that could have been set anywhere in the Middle East. We went through the outer office where a secretary was watching helplessly the constant comings and goings, and marched straight in to see the deputy mayor. Several people were already seated in front of him, but that made no difference; we simply joined them.

On the wall behind Shimon Koubi's desk were hung portraits of Ze'ev Jabotinsky (the founder of hardline Zionism who died in 1940), of Menachem Begin (the former Irgun leader and Likud Prime Minister), and of Yitzhak Shamir (the former underground leader and Likud Prime Minister). These three strong men of Zionism have clearly had a deep influence on his life from his very early years. Shimon Koubi joined Betar, the Zionist youth movement which was inspired by Jabotinsky and abhorred the socialist ideology behind other wings of Zionism, at the age of ten. Three years later he was accepted into Irgun; instructions in the use of weapons were combined with lessons in Jewish history and the ideology of the nationalist movement.

Shimon Koubi remembers clearly the battles for the control of his home town. For six months, he told me, Safed was under siege by Arab forces. From his office he pointed out which parts of the town were under Jewish and which under Arab control, and where the confrontation line was drawn. Across from the municipal offices stands the stark structure of the former British Mandate police station. The iron grilles over the ground-floor windows have rusted, but the exterior of this building, as of many others in Safed, still bears the scars of the fighting in 1948. The British flag was lowered from the roof of that police station and the British pulled out of town on 15 May 1948. Then the battle between the two sides began in earnest. 'Within three weeks,' Shimon Koubi told me, 'everything was finished. The Arabs had all gone to Lebanon.' Forty-five

Jewish fighters had been killed.

Shimon Koubi's overview of Jewish history is shared by Yitzhak Shamir and many other Israelis I met. Safed, he told me, had never been deserted by the Jews in 2,000 years. The Arabs, therefore, were latecomers, interlopers in the homeland of the Jews. Events like the massacres of Jews in Hebron, Tiberias and Safed in 1929, and the hanging in the British military prison in Acre in 1946 of seven members of Irgun from Safed, were simply extra justification, when none was needed, for the fact that the War of Independence and the resulting exodus of the Arab population were themselves natural bricks in the structure of Jewish history. As Shimon Koubi remembers those days, 'the mood was good. We, the Jews, here were few in number; the Arabs were many. Survival was all. We were determined that the events of 1929 would never happen again.'

After the war of independence, Shimon Koubi entered the Herut party which had been founded by his mentor Menachem Begin. And without question he is a member for life. Today, as his sister confirmed, he lives for Likud politics. But as a dedicated Herut purist he laments the fact that in the process of its becoming a big popular political bloc some of the principles and some of the ideology of Herut have been diluted. 'We can hear voices in our party which say Israel can survive by giving up land [in the Occupied Territories].' For Shimon Koubi such talk is heresy, because, like all hawks in Israel, he doesn't believe that there has been a single centimetre of change in Arab attitudes to Israel, despite public indications and official pronouncements to the contrary. 'The attitude of the Arabs today is the same as that before 1948. They want this land. They're not just talking about Judea and Samaria [the West Bank]; they mean Jaffa, Safed, Tiberias . . . As a man who's fought in all the wars of Israel from 1948 until today I can say that nothing has changed in the Arab orientation; the issues are the same as they were before the Balfour Declaration. Yasser Arafat says the Palestinians want the right to come back, which means they want to bring back the 20,000 Arabs to Safed, the 100,000 to Jaffa . . . Sorry, this is impossible.'

Supporters of hard-line attitudes to the Arab world enjoy influential backing. Dr Dore Gold is a leading analyst at the Jaffee Centre for Strategic Studies at Tel Aviv University. In March 1990, following evidence that Iraq was trying to smuggle triggers for nuclear bombs out of Britain, President Saddam Hussein of Iraq threatened to wipe out half of

Israel with chemical weapons if the Israelis launched a pre-emptive strike. In an article published in the immediate wake of this sudden increase in Middle East tension, Dr Gold made the following comment: 'There has been an incorrect assumption, commonly put forward lately, that the Arab world has implicitly accepted Israel's existence in the Middle East.'

The argument of the hawks, therefore, is that the battle may have been won but the war goes on. And the fight must be taken to the enemy. Thus the invasion of Lebanon in 1982; and thus the constant sparring in the war of words between the hawks on both sides of the Middle East conflict. I was often puzzled in Israel by the way assumptions about Arab attitudes and intentions were expressed as cast-iron certainties. One might question the sincerity of, for example, a statement by Yasser Arafat affirming his belief in Israel's right to exist. But could one say with absolute confidence that he was telling a bald lie?

Both sides in the Middle East conflict are prone to this kind of sweeping generalization which is dressed up as logic and fed to a hungry people. Only a few days after my meeting with Shimon Koubi, President Assad of Syria was once again declaring to a youth rally in Damascus that Israel was still seeking a 'greater Israel stretching from the Nile to the Euphrates'. And mirroring the overview of Jewish history espoused by Shimon Koubi and others, the Syrian leader predicted that the tide would eventually flow in favour of the Islamic countries in the Middle East. The opposition to Israel, he vowed, would continue, 'bearing in mind that the time is long and our Jihad [holy war] should be as long as time itself . . . We are just at the beginning.'

President Assad here is borrowing the religious idea of Jihad to justify to his own people his hawkish policies and to try to win support for them. But on both sides of the conflict there are those for whom religion itself is the motivating force for their aggressive attitudes and actions. Islamic fundamentalists aim to topple all 'non-Islamic' regimes in the Middle East; and they include Syria on this list as prominently as Israel. President Assad authorized the elimination of the Muslim Brotherhood movement in Syria by the simple but ruthless expedient of putting to death many thousands of them.

Within Israel there is a strong movement which argues that if it is the will of God for the Jewish people to be in that land, then no other arguments are valid – certainly no arguments about Palestinian nationalism. And, for some Israelis, that means there is no justification for Palestinians' remaining in either Israel or the Occupied Territories. The years I spent in Israel saw the notion of 'transfer', the expulsion of Arabs, being put on to the political agenda by a new extreme right party, Moledet. 'Before that,' Hanoch Smith, a leading pollster and political analyst in Jerusalem, told me, 'the word wasn't in the political vocabulary.' It was hard to believe that this was happening. Here was a state created for the Jews – a people who had suffered centuries of persecution and abuse – giving birth to groups whose agenda included plans for the forcible transportation of families from one land to another.

It was, for a time, tempting to say that despite the emergence of the notion of 'transfer', support for it was limited. But the polls began to tell another story. The first fifteen months of the Intifada (the Arabic word for the uprising by Palestinians in the Occupied Territories which began at the end of 1987) were accompanied by a general softening of attitudes on the part of the Israeli public towards a solution of the Palestinian problem. But then, with the realization that the uprising could not be stamped out overnight, the pattern changed. Palestinian frustration led both to killings within their own communities and attacks on Israelis (like the forcing of 'Bus 405' off the edge of the Tel Aviv to Jerusalem highway in 1989, and the attack on an Israeli tourist bus in Egypt the following year). The upshot was a rise in support for hawkish policies. Towards the end of 1989 Hanoch Smith carried out a poll asking members of the public whether – if political efforts to reach a solution of the Palestinian problem failed – they would consider the policy of 'transfer'. No fewer than fifty-two per cent said 'yes.' Smith's poll indicates that the notion of 'transfer' has become more legitimate at the popular level than the political level, at least for the time being.

The chances of a full and comprehensive settlement of the Palestinian problem in the near future are not good. The more time that passes without such a settlement, the greater the build-up of frustration within the Palestinian communities, both inside and outside the Occupied Territories. Inevitably, in my view, this will mean an increase in desperate acts of violence. Each such act will in turn fuel support for hawkish groups in Israel and provide ammunition for those who argue that compromise spells disaster.

All this comes on top of a noticeable hardening of attitudes among the younger generations of Israelis, whatever their individual backgrounds. Ideals of pioneering Zionism are being replaced in many cases by rank nationalism. Sometimes this is influenced and fuelled by fundamentalist religious doctrines, but not always. Charles S. Liebman, in an article in the *Jerusalem Quarterly* at the end of 1987, commented that:

> according to opinion polls, Jews of Oriental [Asian or African] origin and young people also favour ultra-nationalist policies. When ethnic and age-group status are combined they result in especially extreme attitudes. For example, a May 1985 poll of 15–18-year-olds found that 50 per cent of the Oriental youth, compared with 21 per cent of the Ashkenazi youth, reported they agreed with the ideas which Rabbi Meir Kahane and his Kach party support, ideas which include expelling all Arabs.

Political scientists say that trend has continued. An Israeli girl told me about her experiences on a blind date organized by a friend. As she started chatting with her new companion the subject, inevitably in Israel, came round to politics. It soon became clear that their views were markedly different. The man said he believed the problem of the Arabs could be solved easily if 'we got rid of all the bleeding-heart liberals' in Israel and started taking some tougher measures against the Palestinians. The girl, a self-confessed 'bleeding-heart liberal', realized that there was no potential for a deep relationship here; they would have to agree to differ. But she added that in her view the answer was to give the Palestinians a state on the understanding that Israel would take it back if need be. After all, she concluded, 'they're all human beings.' Her companion disagreed: 'To me they're closer to dogs.'

The thrust of the arguments in favour of 'transfer' differs little from those put forward in the Arab world in the years following the creation of the state of Israel – that the struggle would continue until the Jewish state was driven into the sea. In neither is there room for compassion or compromise. Do the Arabs still nurture such a dream? Some do. But my belief is that the majority probably recognizes, albeit reluctantly, that Israel is there to stay. However, the likelihood of this belief being put to the test appears to wane a little each day, since so many Israelis are still convinced that the views of the Arabs have not changed. And a threat like the one made by President Saddam Hussein in 1990 (to annihilate half of Israel) does not help foster mutual trust. Nor does the proposed expulsion of hundreds of thousands of Palestinians, as advocated by a political group whose influence is growing. In other words, the current trends in Israel, some of which are inter-related to and matched by developments and attitudes in the Arab world, only reinforce the hands of the hawks in the region – Israeli and Arab alike.

The conventional wisdom is that a settlement of the Palestinian problem is the key to breaking the vicious circle. For Israeli ultra-nationalists inspired by a strong belief in the fundamentals of Judaism, the details about what happens to the Palestinian people are negligible compared with the overwhelming importance of the Jewish attachment to the land itself. Moshe Schlass is an ultra-orthodox Jew living in a house with its own courtyard in the Old City of Jerusalem. He's a painter. Large canvases filled with bold swirling colours are hung on the walls. And like his works, Moshe Schlass is larger than life.

He emigrated to Israel from the United States because he wanted to raise his family 'on the most fertile ground possible, in both the physical and spiritual senses'. In his view, 'the creator of the universe has allocated this part of the world, including Judea and Samaria, to be our land . . . Israel belongs to the Jewish people just like America belongs to the American people. If the Italians want to come and take over America, or the Greeks want to do the same, they can't . . . Israel is not a normal situation for world property. It was given to the Jewish people by God himself. And even though over the years everyone tried to wipe it out for whatever reason, it belongs to the Jewish people. Anyone who wants to live here, just like America, has to respect the government. American power was taken by force, they took by force a country that wasn't theirs, they completely took control from those people the country belongs to because they occupied it first, and they signed all kinds of treaties they never kept – and that's OK. Here, this country belongs to us and if anyone wants to live here they have to respect the laws and rules of this country. And unfortunately a lot of Jews are bending over backwards because they have a sense of self-hatred and shame of being Jewish. So they give away their right arm and become a lefty in the process. A lot of people think that by making these compromises they're going to gain something. You know, first of all you don't compromise with a criminal because he has no rights to begin with.'

Among the hawks in Israel there is a fear that the parties on the centre right will be seduced or pressured by the international community into making concessions which would result in territory being surrendered.

Certainly, as Yitzhak Shamir found out when he was Prime Minister of the coalition government of national unity, centre-right leaders can find themselves in uncomfortable positions. Mr Shamir was under pressure from his Labour coalition partners (who had the backing of the United States) to take a more flexible attitude to the search for Middle Eastern peace. At the same time there was equal pressure from within his own Likud party (led by Ariel Sharon) and parties further to the right. His inability to dance to the various tunes that were being played led eventually to the collapse of the government.

His attempts to balance all those pressures pointed up the difficulty that hawks in Israel have in reaching a Middle East settlement. Negotiation means compromise, but political support at home depends on rigid steadfastness. Thus Mr Shamir, addressing a meeting on the subject of the major influx of Soviet Jews in 1990, said that: 'Big immigration requires Israel to be big as well . . . we need all the space [in the Occupied Territories] to house all the people.' This was apparently a clear statement of principle – that the Occupied Territories would always have to be an integral part of Israel. Supporters on the right were delighted. But then, in the face of an international outcry, Shamir tried to soften his statement. What he'd really meant, he said, was that Israel needed to be 'big' only in the sense of 'strong and united'. Did he fool anyone with this double-speak? Not a bit of it. As Arye Naor, a cabinet secretary in a previous Likud government, wrote in the *Jerusalem Post* at the time:

> According to Shamir's political dictionary, 'a strong and united Israel' requires, first of all, a strong determination to act in the national interest. The nation cannot be united unless the national interest is guarded and protected; and that interest means, first of all, that the nation itself must be strong. Since a territorial relinquishment to the enemy could only weaken the nation and strengthen the enemy, Israel should never give the Arabs any territory.

But such assurances do not satisfy all those on the right. In 1988 an international arbitration panel ruled that Israel should hand back to Egypt a tiny enclave at Taba at the northern end of the Red Sea, close to Eilat. The Taba affair had taken on an importance in Israeli-Egyptian relations which was out of all proportion to the size of the strip itself – a tiny area of barren land bordered on the one side by a backdrop of brown, rocky hills and on the other by a few hundred yards of Red Sea beach. Ownership of the strip had been contested since the start of the century, but in recent times it had been part of Egypt before being captured by Israel in the 1967 Middle East War. When Israel withdrew from Sinai in 1982 it hung on to Taba, claiming sovereignty over it and allowing a luxury hotel to be built there. Egypt contested the claim and said that normal relations with Israel would be impossible as long as the dispute remained unsettled. Many Israelis I know never believed that their country's claim to Taba was justified, and there was little surprise when the five-man international arbitration panel in Geneva found in favour of Egypt.

As the news came over the radio from Geneva the owner of a beachside bar wasn't listening. He knew very well what the judgement was going to be. He went on sitting at the bar with a beer in front of him, and with the music of Vivaldi filling the air. But such a fatalistic approach was not adopted by groups on the far right in Israel, supporters of which had gathered with banners in a protest on the one road through the strip. For them the importance of the Taba dispute was not the loss of the luxury hotel or even the loss of the strip itself. Rather, they saw the affair as a lesson about what happens when international bodies become involved in disputes over land between Israel and Arab countries: Israel is forced to make concessions. 'We are afraid that the same thing will happen in respect of the whole of Judea and Samaria [the occupied West Bank] if Israel allows international involvement in the issue,' one of the protesters told me. 'We take Taba as a warning. Likud may speak the same language as us. But if they take the path of negotiations over Judea and Samaria, they'll be forced into accepting the kind of thing that's happening here.'

Two years later supporters of this view felt that their nightmare was beginning to come true. Likud was flirting with the idea of elections in the Occupied Territories, preceded by talks with a Palestinian delegation. For those in the centre and on the left in Israel, the Likud position was hopelessly inflexible and therefore unacceptable – 'an obstacle to peace'. For hawks within Likud and in parties further to the right, though, Likud was already offering far too much; the door was being opened to a process which would inevitably see international pressure being applied until Israel was forced to give up land. Feelings ran so high that a split appeared within Likud. Ariel Sharon resigned from the cabinet, arguing that the government was leading the country down a path to catastrophe.

As the final Israeli pull-out from Taba took place, on an unseasonably blustery and grey spring day by the Red Sea, Israeli hotel workers and right-wing protesters held a noisy and at times hysterical protest, denouncing the Likud government. Scuffles with police ensued. Finally a procession with the Israeli flag at the front snaked past the newly erected Egyptian border gate. The protesters sang the Israeli national anthem in mournful voices as they passed back over the new boundary. Meanwhile, on a dusty mound overlooking the gate, an Egyptian guard of honour were ready to mark the raising of their country's flag. Scores of Egyptian workers scrambled up the mound to watch the ceremony. At the appointed hour, as the flag was raised, a military band started playing the Egyptian national anthem. But the first notes were barely audible before the anthem was drowned by unrestrained and deafening shouts from the crowd of '*Allahu akbar, Allahu akbar*'. The handful of Israelis present looked chilled by this outburst of Muslim and blatantly anti-Israel sentiments ('*Taba today, Tel Aviv tomorrow*', was one of the chants woven through the chorus of '*Allahu akbar*'). In that grey day by the shores of the Red Sea, in the space of a few minutes, a windblown stretch of desert was the stage for a display, in miniature, of Middle Eastern hostilities; Islamic fervour and Israeli nationalism came face to face.

The Islamic chants from the crowd of Egyptian workers, given prominence of course on Israel television that night, did nothing to help those in Israel promoting the cause of dialogue and compromise with the Arabs. After all, it was argued, Egypt had signed a peace treaty with Israel, and if these were the true sentiments of ordinary Egyptians, what could be expected from Syrians, Iraqis or other Arabs? The instinctive distrust of Arabs which one finds among so many Israelis is all the stronger in those whose views are loosely defined as being right of centre. Also there is more of a tendency among this group to see the world outside as inherently hostile to Israel. 'Israelis see peace as meaning a quiet life without any threats of wars.' That is the view of Minna Givton who emigrated to Palestine in 1946. 'The Arabs see peace as more territory, getting back the territory they think they've lost. By talking to individual Arabs I've found that we're not on the same wavelength at all about what peace is. From two such different premises I wonder where we could meet? They know they can't kick us into the sea, but they can make our life as uncomfortable as they're doing now. To say that Arabs have beaten the Israeli army [in the uprising in the Occupied Territories], to say they've shown what brave, unarmed people can do, is rubbish. Because one could do what foreign armies do: mow down the first few rows and that would settle it. But nobody is going to do that, and so you go on getting a reputation throughout the world of not being reasonable.'

Misunderstanding and lack of sympathy on the part of the outside world, confusion and doubts within Israel about the future – in such an atmosphere the arguments for building even tougher battlements around the fortress state seem irrefutable to many Israelis. 'If we allow a Palestinian state to be created in the Occupied Territories,' one middle-aged Israeli lady told me, 'we'd need to start learning how to swim better in the Mediterranean.' And Israelis who express such views do not want to be criticized by Jews or non-Jews in the world outside. Especially by non-Jews. A Likud Knesset member Uzi Landau was asked in an interview about the hypothetical case of a liberal Jew in the United States who sincerely believed that unless Israel negotiated with the PLO the Jewish state would cease to exist. What should that Jew do, the interviewer wondered; keep quiet? 'He doesn't have to keep quiet,' Uzi Landau replied, 'but he should express his views in closed, Jewish forums and through the existing channels of communications with the state of Israel.'

I found an explanation for the emergence of this kind of attitude among those on the right in an article by Professor Leslie Susser in the *Jerusalem Post*. There was always, he wrote, an inner dialectical struggle in Zionism between humanism and nationalism.

> Israel would inculcate a fierce national pride – while imparting at the same time a respect for a universal humanism that transcended national boundaries . . . The dichotomy was accentuated after 1967. Nationalist Israel pushed for annexation of the Territories, humanist Israel for their return. The rise of Likud and Messianic religious fervour led to a greater sense of national particularism. In its narrowest form, it fuelled a parochialism, and the 'world is against us' philosophy.

Once this kind of philosophy takes root – whether in Israel, or in Syria or Iraq – it's very hard to get rid of it. And rather than seeking ways of building bridges to the world outside, the inhabitants of the Middle East fortress states put up fresh barriers and look inwards. Here, for example, is the Likud Knesset member Moshe Arens speaking shortly after he had been appointed Foreign Minister in the Shamir government: 'Israel needs secure borders in this most dangerous part of the world where we are facing who knows what weapons . . . We don't need advice from anyone . . . but just need to remember some basic geographical facts. We are aghast when we see the world's "great" lining up to pay homage to Yasser Arafat, waiting to be photographed shaking his hand. It will take historians to explain this most unusual phenomenon. It's incomprehensible to me . . . Israel is the country that has had to fight for its life almost every year.'

Fighting for survival or keeping in readiness in case such a fight should be necessary are constant strains on Israel's budget. Israel would have no chance of coping with those strains if billions of dollars' worth of United States aid were not forthcoming each year. From the viewpoint of the United States Israel is a special friend: Washington is committed to making sure of Israel's survival, and there are close links between Israel and the Jewish community in the United States. Also, Israel is a dependable strategic ally in an unstable region. Such allies are needed, it is argued in Washington, both to protect Western interests in the Middle East and to block the spread of Soviet influence. That, at least, used to be the argument before the easing of super-power tensions which accompanied the emergence of democratic movements in the Soviet Union and the countries of Central and Eastern Europe at the start of the 1990s.

The first observation made in Israel was that the tide of democracy spreading over Europe was not going to reach the Middle East. The second related to how the super-powers might view the region in the light of the relaxation in tension between Moscow and Washington. If the two giants no longer looked at the region in terms of rivalry over spheres of influence, what need would there be for strategic allies there? And what would be the point of committing so many resources to those allies?

Benjamin Netanyahu is one of the most prominent voices of the right in Israel. He served as his country's ambassador to the United Nations and later was Israel's deputy Foreign Minister. His smooth, American-accented and eminently quotable English, matched with his debonair looks, made him a natural spokesman for the Likud-led government in which he served. In his capacity as a member of the government he used the Information Division of the Foreign Ministry to circulate his thoughts on 'Israel in the era of thaw'. He observed correctly that Israel's political history had been 'intertwined with the reality of the Cold War', and commented that while Israel would welcome a reduction in Soviet support 'for the radical regimes and organizations in the Arab world that have led the struggle against us', this development would also weaken Soviet leverage. 'This restraining effect may come to an end when the USSR ceases its active involvement in the Middle East as the Americans' rival. The termination of this involvement may also catalyse increasing pressure in the US to reduce, gradually or quickly, American involvement in Middle East conflicts. Consequently Israel may find itself in un-splendid isolation against military coalitions of Arab states.'

It was fitting that Benjamin Netanyahu should choose a literally hawkish image to highlight the climax of his assessment of the thaw in super-power relations. 'Is there any doubt', he asked, 'that if we dispose of our military deterrent the Arab nations will swoop like vultures in search of prey, even if they signed peace agreement with us?'

Once again there is expressed the absolute certainty that the Arab states are bent on the destruction of Israel. No Israeli would question the need for the country to maintain both a high level of alert and an effective ability to deter attacks from the Arab world, just as no Syrian (or any other Arab) would question the sentiments of the Syrian Foreign Minister, Farouq al-Sharaa, when he said: 'We are sure that the main reason for tension in the region is the expansionist policies of Israel and the huge stocks of nuclear and chemical weapons which are kept by Israel.'

A frightening cocktail is being mixed in the region: chemical and nuclear weapons are being developed by the leaders, while religious and nationalist fanaticism are beginning to take root among the peoples. In the occupied West Bank I have listened to Israeli settlers talking about plans to set up the independent state of Judea if a government in Jerusalem should agree to give up a single square inch of, as they see it, the land given by God to the Jewish people. The notion of a 'state of Judea' might seem comical to outsiders, but sections of the settlers, who are well armed and well organized, are prepared to fight for what they believe in, and if need be, to spill Jewish blood. Likud Knesset member Uzi Landau, who opposes territorial compromise as passionately as anyone in Israel, recognizes that there is 'a danger that if a decision is made to withdraw from Judea and Samaria [the West Bank], there might be hundreds of thousands of Israelis taking the law into their own hands. I am not proposing that all necessary measures should not be taken against them – but a wise statesman will be careful to avoid such a situation. As much as Israel's history may have been "intertwined with the reality of the Cold War", its future, I believe will be intertwined with both the arms race and the spread of hardline, fundamentalist thinking in the Middle East.'

Islamic fundamentalism provided much of the impetus for the start of the Palestinian uprising in the Occupied Territories in December 1987. It is no coincidence that the flames of the rebellion were lit, not in the West Bank but in the Gaza Strip, and it is still in Gaza that the spirit of the uprising can be felt most keenly. When you arrive in the Strip the apparent hopelessness of it all crowds in on you. And it doesn't take long to understand why Islamic fundamentalism should flourish in this compost-heap of despair.

You can read about Islamic fundamentalism in textbooks – but you can learn much more in a brief encounter with a family like the Mabhouhs. I came across them, all forty members, as they were whiling away the time waiting for their house to be blown up by the Israeli army. Their house, before it was demolished, stood on a slight hill on the edge of the Jebaliya refugee camp, the biggest camp in the Gaza Strip where some 60,000 people have lived for decades in small breeze-block shelters. Bits of plastic sacking attached to roofs and walls flapped in the wind. Weak spring sunshine had made little headway in drying the sticky winter mud.

The Mabhouh family had removed everything from their house and assembled at a half-finished building a few hundred yards away. Women and children were sprawled on the grass outside, the menfolk were on the roof. They were about to have a meal and wouldn't hear of my not joining them. So I squatted down with the others on a straw mat and shared their chicken and rice. I realized gradually that there was something wrong with this scene. Occasionally one of the men would glance over to watch the army continuing preparations for the demolition of their house, but in general the appetites were hearty. There was no tension and no anger – rather, an incredible sense of calm resignation.

The story of the Mabhouhs was that one of the brothers had been accused of killing an Israeli soldier. He was never caught, but for weeks the Israeli army harassed the family, believing that they were hiding him. On one occasion the whole family was put into an army truck and told they were being deported to Lebanon. For hours they were driven around, only to be deposited eventually back home. In the end, it turned out that the brother had managed to flee the country, so, as collective punishment for the family, the army decided to destroy their house.

The men were smiling for much of the time as they told me their story. They said they were proud of what had happened; it had brought honour to the family. 'The Israelis', one of them continued, 'think that by blowing up our house they'll break our determination. They think we're like them, that if we lose something material we'll get upset. But for us it's no great importance. Allah teaches us that we must be patient. Patience is part of our faith.' And he quoted a verse from the Qu'ran to back up his point.

Mahmoud, the brother on the run, was a member of Hamas, the underground Islamic movement which enjoys very widespread support in the Occupied Territories. It developed out of the Muslim Brotherhood organizations which the Israeli authorities encouraged in the late 1970s and early '80s to try to weaken support for the PLO. Hamas is not interested in negotiating with Israel for the establishment of an independent Palestinian state; it wants an Islamic state, as the saying goes, 'from the river to the sea' – from the Jordan to the Mediterranean. In other words, Hamas wants the removal of Israel.

Another group in the Occupied Territories, Islamic Jihad, sees itself as part of a wider movement aimed at the overthrow of all non-Islamic regimes in the Middle East. Inspiration and finance come in part from Iran and the Iranian-backed Shiite organization in Lebanon, Hizbollah.

It is often said that the Palestinians are running out of patience at the lack of progress in the search for peace in the Middle East. But despair is breeding patience of another kind: a cold and determined patience inspired by Islam. If the attitudes of the Mabhouh family are anything to go by, both Israel and the mainstream of the PLO may have cause to be alarmed. As Avraham Burg, a Labour Knesset member, commented: 'If we don't talk to the PLO today, we'll talk to Hamas tomorrow.' In other words, better the Devil you know than the Devil you don't.

But that's the view of a leading Israeli dove.

CHAPTER FIVE

The doves

THE 1982 Israeli war in Lebanon was in full swing when Dudik Ohana joined the ranks of the doves. One event triggered this new outlook. It was something akin to a religious conversion, a psychological change that took place deep in the man's soul and which will not easily be erased. From that moment, he says, he knew that, whatever the solution to the problems of the Middle East might be, as far as he was concerned war was no longer an option.

Dudik Ohana and I sat at a table in his fish restaurant by the edge of the Sea of Galilee. It was an evening in winter, so trade was slack. Dudik Ohana had time to talk about the events which changed his life. He spoke slowly and thoughtfully, his hands sometimes groping for the right words in English. Ohana still has the mannerisms of his Moroccan forebears, even though he was born in Israel. The family have long been associated with the fish industry around the Lake, at one time exporting their catch to Beirut and Damascus. That was, of course, decades before 1982 and Operation Peace for Galilee, or, as it is more commonly and properly described, the war in Lebanon.

In that war Dudik Ohana served as a paratrooper, working mainly with helicopters moving troops and weapons from one position to another. At times the passengers were wounded soldiers. His base was at Rosh Pina in northern Israel close to a major hospital. The casualties from the war were brought there before being sent, if necessary, for treatment elsewhere in the country.

One day while he was at Rosh Pina word came that a major mistake had been made: Israeli planes had attacked a convoy of their own men in Lebanon. Ohana and another officer were off duty at the base at the time; but when the wounded from the incident were brought in, they went to see if extra help was needed. The rotors from the giant helicopter were creating a strong wind as the doors were opened, and troops rushed in to carry out stretcher-cases. Those who could manage to walk did so. Among the latter was a lonely figure – a military rabbi. As he walked away the wind blew off the blanket that had been wrapped around him, revealing severe burns on his naked body. But his prayer shawl was still around his neck, and he tried to pull it down to cover his nakedness. Meanwhile the injured were being separated – Israelis one side, Arabs the other – and so were the dead bodies. Ohana remembers a voice calling out: 'Here, take this one, it's one of ours.'

This simple scene at Rosh Pina counts for little when matched against the bloodshed, emotional strain or acts of barbarism committed during the war in Lebanon. But Ohana says this single occasion, this one small experience, opened his eyes for the first time. And he knew he would never be the same again. 'I could see very clearly that this was madness. When you've seen madness you don't need to to ask any more questions. We have to find peace. I've seen the alternative so clearly with my eyes and my soul.' Shortly after this incident Ohana left the country. He had no choice, he said, but to get away, to live somewhere peaceful for a while.

The war in Lebanon was a turning-point for many Israelis. An American-born Professor of Indian Studies at the Hebrew University in Jerusalem said he still dreams of war because of his experience then. It was 'probably the most traumatic experience in my life. Mostly because I was totally opposed to it. I thought it was a stupid war. As a combat medic I saw people die – that terrible sense that it's all for nothing.'

But for that Professor the Lebanon War was merely one more example of Israel proceeding in a manner which was not to his liking. As a youth he was a committed Zionist; he learned Hebrew in the United States. He came to Israel in 1967, the year of the Middle East War, but had been planning to come anyway. 'It was a happy time to come, by comparison with today,' he recalled. 'Today I feel like it's a different country.' For four years in the early 1970s the Professor and his wife were out of Israel. They returned 'to the old Israel and watched it crumble in front of our eyes as if a nightmare had started. We're left-wing, Peace Now, the usual Israeli academic intellectual stuff, and we're appalled at what's happened. This is an Israel that's autistic, and thinks of itself and the rest of the world as being in polar opposition – us and them. It's an antagonistic universe in which in terms of political culture there's this self-righteous vision of the place – the Jews are right and the rest of the world is wrong.'

Orielle Berry came to Israel from South Africa, and also remembers the happy atmosphere of those days. 'It had quite an impact on me. There was a lot of euphoria about all the territories that had been occupied. I don't think that people at the time realized what was really happening. You know, there was such a feeling of "We've made it, despite all the odds against us" that I don't think they realized the implications of occupying all the territories.'

But like so many Israelis, Orielle Berry pinpoints the war in Lebanon as a turning-point in the thinking of a large section of the population. 'The Lebanon War was the crystallizing factor for a complete evaporation of idealism. It was when some Israelis, for the first time, refused to serve in the army. They didn't see it as a people's army but as an army of conquerors committing acts that they didn't want to be party to, like the siege of Beirut. I think that Sabra and Chatila [the Palestinian refugee camps on the edge of Beirut where close to a thousand men, women and children were massacred by Lebanese Christian militiamen under the noses of the Israeli army] was a major event that destroyed a lot of idealism and created tremendous rifts in Israeli society.'

For those of us unfortunate enough to have been inside Beirut during the siege by the Israeli army, the chief consideration was keeping alive under the constant barrages from the land, sea and sky. While I remember hearing about the development of a peace protest movement in Israel, it was not something one could take very seriously on the ground in Beirut. It is only having spent time in Israel afterwards that I see the extent to which those events traumatized a large section of society. On one occasion in a social discussion with Israelis the subject came round to the war in Lebanon. One of those present had served in the air force at that time. 'The way we used to bomb Beirut during the siege,' he said, 'it's a wonder that anyone survived.' When I told him that we had been among those sheltering from his bombs he became silent. Until that moment, I believe, he hadn't wanted to think of there being any human beings in the city whom one day he would meet. Looking at war as a conflict at arm's distance was that man's way of coping with the emotional strain. For the average Israeli soldier in the field and for the Palestinian guerillas, that option was not available.

Leading the way into the Lebanese quagmire was the Likud Defence Minister, Ariel Sharon. He deceived the public, who were told that a limited military operation was under way – but more important than that, he deceived the rest of the government. When the public realized that they had been kept in the dark, hundreds of thousands of them took to the streets in protest. 'Peace Now' became the slogan, and the organization bearing that name grew in popularity.

Being a dove in Israel is no easy task. Selling peace is difficult in a country that was involved in five wars in its first forty years of existence and that feels threatened by the overwhelming forces surrounding it. Sitting in Jerusalem one June evening my gaze was drawn to three leaves of an exotic plant in the garden next door. The leaves were coarse in texture and shaped like swords pointing into the sky, and they were caught as if in a spotlight by the slanting rays of the evening sun. They reminded me of the jagged memorials to battles which are dotted on hillsides all over the country. Keeping memories alive is an Israeli obsession.

Earlier on that June day Israel had celebrated the anniversary of the fall of East Jerusalem from Jordanian hands in the Middle East War of 1967. Larger-than-life Israeli flags had flanked the pathway leading to the Six Day War memorial on Givat Hamivtar (Ammunition Hill) where some of the fiercest battles had been fought, and where the defensive trenches of the Jordanian army have been left as a frozen reminder of the conflict and the eventual Israeli victory. Two or three small Palestinian houses still stand in the area around the memorial. As the crowds of visitors, many of them children, made their way from parked cars and coaches towards the memorial, I noticed that washing was hanging on a clothes line in the scruffy little yard outside one of the houses. Who, on this day, was intruding on whom, I wondered.

The Holocaust of the Jews of Europe during World War Two under Nazi rule, above all, is the main event colouring the judgement of any Israeli contemplating taking a path towards peace. (Even as I was completing this chapter the phone rang – it was a group called 'Lapid', meaning 'Torch', which is dedicated to 'transmitting the lessons of the Holocaust', inviting me to a public 'trial' of Britain and the United States for not bombing the concentration camps.) Natural fear based on tragic and catastrophic historical experience? Or a psychological chain around the ankles of the country, preventing it moving forward towards peace? Both.

Many complicated and emotional pressures push and pull on the conscience of the average Israeli as he tries to make up his mind about what the best course for his country should be. Experts and ambitious political figures exploit these pressures without shame. The pressures are grounded in memories – of the Holocaust, of the battles for the creation of the state of Israel, of the subsequent wars with the Arabs, of the disaster in Lebanon; or they are associated with external fears – of future conflicts, of the build-up of weapons in the region, or even of growing international isolation. For all these reasons, fighting an election campaign on a peace platform will never be easy, even if peace concerns just the occupied West Bank and Gaza Strip, and the future relationship with the Palestinians. 'Not one inch of territory' is a clear and unambiguous slogan which is easy to sell because it plays on the emotional insecurity that most Israelis feel about the threat from the Arabs as a whole. A slogan like 'Talks with the Palestinians (possibly the PLO, possibly not) leading to the surrender of (some) occupied land in exchange for peace, provided that the necessary guarantees are forthcoming, etc etc . . .' is a mouthful, and it also has a basic flaw in the opinion of many Israelis: it is an uncharted, and therefore dangerous path on which to set out.

Clear examples of the split within Israeli society over the future of the Occupied Territories can be seen every time an election is held or an opinion poll is published. But a more concrete and more colourful illustration of the split can be seen every week on the streets of Jerusalem. One o'clock on a Friday afternoon is a busy time in all the cities of Israel as the population heads home for the weekend. At this time a group of women, dressed totally in black and carrying black cardboard-cut-out hands on which are written *End the occupation*, gather in a square in the centre of Jewish West Jerusalem. They stand silently in a circle. Around them there is anything but silence: above the grinding roar of the rush-hour traffic abuse is heaped on them from passers-by on foot, from motorists in their cars, and from passengers calling out of the windows of buses: 'Arafat's whores!' 'Go and sleep with Arafat!' 'You're a load of black vermin!'

The 'Women in Black' say they will go on putting up with the abuse because it is essential to continue to remind people of the evils, as they see them, of the occupation. 'We were nine women in the beginning,' Anat Hoffman told me. 'We are now 2,000, demonstrating in more than twenty locations. It's a very gradual change because we have to overcome an irrational fear. Maybe outsiders can't understand how immense our fears are. And I think Israel will take its first feeble steps towards overcoming this fear soon. But only to understand us you must understand our fears from the Holocaust, and from the fact that when the Arabs say they'll throw us into the sea we believe them. Because this has happened to us. Every woman here has a family album and in the first pages you will see members of the family who've been exterminated in Europe. When you have so many people and all of them have had this scar, then there's a great fear to overcome. Also our Palestinian neighbours have to overcome some of their prejudices about Israelis and about Jews. When both of us can overcome our fears we can sit down and talk. It will be a long haul. But there is no alternative; horrible things are happening.'

The kind of counter-arguments that peace campaigners face in Israel are voiced in their crudest form each Friday lunch-time in Jerusalem by a demonstration against the 'Women in Black' held by a small but vociferous group calling itself 'The Victims of Arab Terror'. One of the counter-demonstrators, an elderly man with a strong New York accent, could not conceal his anger as he spoke to me: 'We're here to protest the black widows, they are traitors to the land of Israel. They think by giving up land they'll have peace, but the Arabs want it all. And these sick black widows are traitors. They supply the rocks that kill our soldiers here. They help the enemy.' And a woman added: 'We want the world to know that rocks kill. Rocks killed little Rami Haver eight years old. You never hear about that. You only hear about Israel on television with the so-called aggressive stand or doing something against the youths. These youths kill people with their rocks. And they have the media and the freedom-rock as their *raison d'être*.'

The arguments over the future of the Occupied Territories relate in part to security, in part to humanistic considerations for ordinary Palestinians and in part also to basic attitudes towards Arabs. On the first point there is a strong argument (and one that has a ready appeal to many Israelis) – because the Arab forces are collectively so superior in number, if not in quality, Israel has no choice but to hang on to every square inch of land. In the event of an invasion, it is argued, the West Bank would be a piece of ground that would buy vital time for Israel: any army crossing the River Jordan, 1,000 feet below sea-level, would face the prospect of climbing a total of some 3,000 feet up to Jerusalem. This would give Israel time to mobilize the reserves and move troops eastwards from the main population centres on the coast to confront the invading army. Strategically located settlements on hilltops in the West Bank, meanwhile, would go into action cutting roads and generally harassing and hindering the progress of the invaders.

But a counter-argument is that the occupation of the West Bank for such strategic reasons has to be weighed against the moral cost of the occupation. A number of highly respected reserve generals and other senior military men believe that with the use of sophisticated early-warning equipment, and in a theatre of war where long-range weapons would probably play a bigger role than in the past, the value of such a strip of land is miniscule when measured against the moral and financial cost of the occupation.

A problem too is that the 'cost' of the occupation is not quantifiable. It can be argued that, after a period of several months in which the army didn't know how to respond to the Palestinian uprising, the rebellion is now being kept within manageable bounds. But Professor Emmanuel Silvan of the Hebrew University of Jerusalem is one of those who believe that Israel must quickly do something about the occupation. He spelt out his views in Ha'aretz newspaper:

> As a result of the Six Day War, to its disadvantage, Israel found itself in . . . an almost classic colonial situation, with one society ruling over another within the same territory, where members of each group have their own common ethnic origin based on culture, collective memory and (in our case) also on a different religion.

Professor Silvan argues that the Palestinian uprising has simply brought matters to a head. He agrees that, despite the widespread outbreaks of violence in the uprising, Israeli

> military superiority and control over the territories remained intact. The Palestinians do not have . . . any suitable military response . . . What has changed in the military sphere is the high cost of continued control: in dead and wounded among the security forces and Jewish civilians, in the heavy load of reserve duty and the especially wearing nature of that job, in tension between the security forces and the judicial authorities, in the increase in the number of 'exceptions' [a code word in this context for physical abuses and killings] and in harm

done to the morale of the soldiers; and we have not yet touched on the price in money of the army's activity in the West Bank and Gaza . . .

After two years and more of the Intifada, most Israelis I met were of the opinion that it had become something they could live with. They would have preferred that it wasn't going on; and knew that the question of what to do about the Palestinian question was exposing serious rifts within Israeli society. But the level of violence, compared with the early days, was down and international attention (a major factor in Israeli thinking) had shifted elsewhere. There were other outcomes – like the fact that for the overwhelming majority of Israelis East Jerusalem had once again become a no-go area, as had the Occupied Territories – no more Sabbath excursions to market in Bethlehem. But otherwise it was nothing too serious.

But this attitude worries peace campaigners like Mordechai Bar'on, once a distinguished senior army officer and now a leading figure in Peace Now. 'At the beginning what was happening in the uprising was shocking,' he told me in his home in Jerusalem, 'but how long can one be shocked?' It's a cruel phenomenon that you can see throughout history – that all generations get used to things that are of a low-drama level: one killed, two killed, three killed. But every day now for hundreds of days. How long can one be shocked? Some of us are. And I'm shocked every morning, and many of us are sensitive enough to not forget that it is a shocking situation. But generally speaking, that is the nature of things.' Despite the numbing effect of the continuing violence, Mordechai Bar'on believes that the uprising has set the stage for an eventual settlement of the Palestinian problem. 'People are not shocked but people know for sure that something else will happen, that we can not continue the occupation, and that in spite of the fact that the Intifada is not threatening on a day-to-day basis, sooner or later the world will not allow us to continue and that there must be a change. Of course not all of us think this: the right-wing still believe that they have a chance to keep the *status quo*. Polls have shown that many, many more people advocate talking to the PLO, which is a great revolution in public opinion in Israel.'

The status of the PLO in the minds of the Israeli public has shifted in recent years. Early in my tour of duty in Israel, towards the end of 1987, I recall a member of the Likud party being stripped of office simply for having met with prominent Palestinians from the Occupied Territories.

At that time any mention of the PLO was considered almost heresy. Two years later Ezer Weizman was being stripped of his place in the inner cabinet by the Likud Prime Minister Yitzhak Shamir for alleged contacts with the organization. And yet a few weeks after that, the man who had been accused of aiding Israel's bitterest enemy was back in the cabinet, albeit in a less influential capacity. Little wonder that the Israeli public was confused. In a matter of years, just as 'transfer' had nudged its way on to the political agenda from the far right, so the idea of talking to the PLO was becoming an acceptable subject for debate, if not an accepted principle, in the mainstream of politics. Younger figures within the Israeli Labour party, like Yossi Beilin, were prepared to declare their views publicly. 'I believe that without the PLO there will be no solution to the conflict. Therefore negotiations with the PLO are inevitable.' And another doveish Labour Knesset member, Avraham Burg, pointed out that after two years of Intifada there were more governments and capitals which recognized the PLO than there were states and regimes which recognized the state of Israel. International reality had changed radically – to Israel's disadvantage.

A third Labour Knesset member, David Liba'i, expressed the view that the law forbidding contact with members of the PLO was not only absurd but harmful to Israel's own interests. He gave an example of what happened during a visit to China. There he had seen a bulletin of news broadcast in English on television whose first item was a report on a visit to Peking by Yasser Arafat. The second told of the imprisonment of Abie Nathan, a leading Israeli peace campaigner who is vainly seeking to legitimize dialogue between Israel and the Palestinians. 'Clearly', Liba'i concluded, 'the "discredited" party wasn't the PLO, but Israel.'

'No more war, no more bloodshed' – Menachem Begin uttered those optimistic (but almost comically unrealistic) words at the time of the signing of the peace treaty between Israel and Egypt. The words are part of a jingle played after the hourly news broadcast on 'The Voice of Peace' – a radio station situated 'somewhere in the Mediterranean' and owned by Abie Nathan. Whether or not the music and the messages of peace have prevented a single drop of blood being spilled in the region is debatable, but the continued existence of the radio station is a measure of the dedication of its colourful and outspoken owner. Abie Nathan has consistently argued that Israel has no choice but to make peace with its neighbours, and that that process means sitting down and talking with the enemy: in this case, the PLO. And the different fates suffered by Abie Nathan and Ezer Weizman (who could not be prosecuted because of parliamentary immunity) as a result of their contacts with the PLO did not go unnoticed among the Israeli public. Not that Abie Nathan was repentant: he said he broke the law deliberately to show how absurd it was. While serving his six-month sentence he said he intended to go on ignoring the law, and soon after his release he was reported to be having another meeting with Yasser Arafat.

Without any question, the inability of the two parties, Israel and the PLO, to find a way of sitting down together has been the biggest obstacle in the search for Middle East peace. Every other attempt has been shown up for what it is: a side-step of the real issue. The PLO was slow in saying publicly and unequivocally that it accepted the reality of Israel's existence within the pre-1967 borders; Israel continues to reject the thesis that the PLO is the only body representing the widest interests within the Palestinian community. It is a classic Middle Eastern paralysis of outlook. Already, radicals within the PLO are calling the tune more and more, and hawks in Israel are growing in strength (clear evidence of this was the formation of the right-wing coalition government in June 1990). The origin of this trend can be traced to the years of wasted opportunity resulting from inflexible positions on both sides of the Middle East conflict.

While in prison, Abie Nathan wrote a letter to a friend in the United States. It was published in the *New York Times*. 'Something terrible', he said, 'has happened to my country. This is not the country I knew when I came here in 1948. We have lost our values. There is nothing humanistic or Jewish in our actions. Without any leadership we are just drifting and may any day enter a storm that could create havoc.'

There is a strong feeling among Israeli doves that the 'storm' could arise from the actions of Israeli settlers who, on a number of occasions since the start of the Intifada in the Occupied Territories, have taken the law into their own hands, acting against both Palestinians and at times the Israeli army. I have heard Israelis of many varying political outlooks express the fear that the day could come when Jew would take up arms against Jew in the Occupied Territories. 'I think the only idealism that exists here', a disaffected young Israeli told me, 'is with people who come here for religious reasons, who feel their tie with the land, people who live in the West Bank and Gaza Strip.' And as every Israeli knows from the experience of the fiercely idealistic Zionist settlers who, against many odds, succeeded in setting up the Jewish state, Jews are prepared to fight to the death for their ideals.

The unilateral actions of the settlers caused sufficient consternation among the doves in Israeli society for a rally to be held by Peace Now in Tel Aviv in the summer of 1989. As politicians and prominent Israelis associated with the peace movement addressed the gathering from a microphone on the stage, it was part of my job as a reporter to mingle with the crowd of several thousands on that warm and sticky evening, and collect the views of some of those present. 'We are against violence and for dialogue with the Palestinians. We want to finish once and for all with this fascism and radicalism which have brought us to the darkest hours of our history,' was the comment of one middle-aged lady. Her husband carried on: 'I think it's awful what we're doing to the Palestinians. The actions of the settlers are against the law.' And comments from others in the crowd continued in this vein: 'We're protesting against the actions of the settlers, their actions against the Arabs and the IDF. They're doing things that people inside Israel wouldn't dare to do. I'm afraid that the future of Israel is in danger . . . People are here in their thousands because they think that the future of Israel is more important than the Occupied Territories . . . We're protesting against the small group of hooligans and fascists who're endangering our principles of democracy and who are acting against the whole spirit of Judaism . . . I'm totally afraid of what's happening on the streets, how people are getting to be extreme, terrorized by terror. I'm afraid for the country, that it's getting lost. Really there's a virus of extremism in Israel.'

Late that night, driving back up to the cooler air of Jerusalem, I realized fully for the first time the extent to which Israeli society had become polarized. My journey home took me close to the Knesset where a few days previously I had recorded other 'vox pop' interviews – this time with a group of settlers who were conducting a protest of their own. Their collective views were summed up by one young man in an open-necked white shirt and with a blue and white kippa (skull cap) on his head. As he leant over a police barrier, a banner in one hand, he told me in a strong American accent: 'Look, the Arabs don't want peace; the Arabs don't like the Jews in Israel. Judea and Samaria [the occupied West Bank] are part of Israel. So the Arabs will have to go. Sooner or later, I'm sorry, they'll have to go.'

Perhaps the 'virus of extremism' is not more than healthy pluralism: democracy at work? In part this is true. But in my view it is more serious: the polarization of society is leading to an erosion of liberalism. It is happening in the Israeli press, as I mentioned earlier – the three years during which I worked in Israel saw a tightening of restrictions on the press in the Occupied Territories, a drift that is camouflaged both by the big overlap between the overseas and local press corps and the overlap between reporting in Israel proper, which is governed by civilian law, and in the Territories, which are under military administration. The problem was well summarized by Pnina Lahav, Professor of Law at Boston University, writing in *Israeli Democracy* magazine:

Palestinian newspapers, in contrast to Israeli newspapers, must submit all of their material to the censor, including recipes, advertisements and obituaries. Often the Palestinian press is denied the right to publish what has already been disseminated in the Hebrew press. Books easily obtainable in Israel are prohibited in the Territories . . . The reality of segregated systems of expression, one relatively free and the other totally restricted, gravely affects both Israeli democracy and the Palestinians in the Territories. The Palestinians, who were denied a free press under King Hussein's rule prior to 1967, have come to relish it. They see how democracy works, the pleasures of thinking and writing, and they desire the same for themselves. Ironically, the democratic freedoms in Israel are in themselves causes of the Intifada, and cannot be changed unless Israeli democracy sacrifices itself on the altar of territorial retention.

At the same time, Israelis are getting used to practising suppression. As masters of the Territories, they not only become masters of the art of stifling freedom of the press, they build a whole support system which teaches them that they are doing the right thing. On more than one occasion the Supreme Court of Israel ruled that the same suppression that is anathema to Israel is perfectly legitimate in the Territories . . . One must wonder about the damage that a twenty-two-year occupation does to those administering it, and about what kind of civic education it gives to a substantial portion of Israelis. The true and overriding danger of the segregated system of suppression and freedom is that the suppression will spill over and flood the freedom within the Green Line.

There are voices even among the doves in Israel which call for greater restrictions to be put on reporting from the Occupied Territories, because of the old idea that the press was a catalyst for the Palestinian uprising. The subject came up once at a party attended by broadly liberal Israelis. 'By allowing foreign correspondents to report freely in the Occupied Territories we're not doing ourselves any favours,' one of those present commented. 'Syria and Iraq get away with whatever they want. It's easier for them. It ought to be the same for us.' But wouldn't that mean Israel coming into line with the illiberal attitudes to the press that prevail in the Middle East? 'So be it,' was his reply.

'It's not the press coverage that's at fault,' another member of the group chipped in. 'The fault is the occupation. The occupation itself is worse for Israel than the press coverage. We should give back the Occupied Territories, and be ready to take them over again if need be.'

But aside from security concerns about the Occupied Territories and aside from humanistic attitudes to the Palestinians there still remains the third point – about basic attitudes between Israelis and Arabs, one to another. What is the use of Israeli doves calling for peace if no one in the region as a whole is echoing their words? Among Israeli doves whom I met I still found an ambivalence in attitudes towards Arabs, even though it was nothing like as pronounced as among the hawks. Orielle Berry, for example, believes that talks should begin with the PLO, and lead to the creation of a Palestinian state in the West Bank, with provisions for Israel's security. Did she believe then, that Arabs as a whole no longer wanted to destroy Israel? 'It's still a fear of mine that they want to destroy us. Every time there's a terror act there's so much splintering among the Arabs. I say we should talk to the PLO, but there are so many groups within that organization. And now Hamas is strong. I do have doubts.'

Shulamit Berger, who's in her sixties, was born in Belgium. A grand piano fills the living-room of her flat in Jerusalem. She's a piano teacher, an active civil rights campaigner, and a member of Peace Now: 'I used to go demonstrating long before Peace Now was founded. The first time was in 1965 against the expropriation of Arab land in Israel.' She also believes that a state should eventually be created for the Palestinians. But again, does she think Arab attitudes to Israel have changed? 'I don't know the Arabs enough to say whether they are changing or not, and of course the Palestinians with whom I associate are liberals with moderate views. But my general feeling is that if I meet a Palestinian per se,' and here she laughs ruefully, 'he doesn't like us. There's a repugnance. I'm quite sure that if we knew each other we might like or dislike one another. But without this happening there's a stigma which is very hard to break.'

The chances of Arabs and Israelis getting to know one another do not look promising. While there is a growing acceptance that Israel's presence in the region is now a part of life, there is no enthusiasm to embrace it. Even within Egypt (the one Arab state linked to Israel by a peace treaty) one finds an attitude, both at official and street levels, which is at best unenthusiastic about the Jewish state. Peace movements as such would not be tolerated in Arab countries even if there was a desire on the part of the populations to create them.

Clearly, if the chains of suspicion and mistrust are to be broken encouragement from outside will be needed. But here again, Israel and the Arab countries are locked in a collective mistrust of the motives of outsiders. The United States is reckoned to be the power most able to bring influence and pressure to bear, but Washington's close links with Israel have led a number of Arab leaders to dismiss the US as a potential honest broker in the region. And within Israel there is also a deep suspicion of outside involvement. Even among doves, there's a feeling that Israel is misunderstood by the outside world, therefore anything which is decided by the international community might not have Israel's genuine interests and security at heart. Pamela Aboulafia, who has lived in Israel for forty years, is a Labour supporter. 'I've always been liberal [at that time part of the right-wing Likud bloc] but I veer towards the Labour Party because they have a more positive approach to peace. I feel our main objective must be peace. I'm voting for the lesser of two evils – it's not a very positive outlook.' Pamela Aboulafia is in favour of talking to the PLO, or anyone, to advance the search for peace. She believes, though, that Israel's true position is misunderstood, partly because of the country's image abroad. 'Our image is very bad, not justifiably so. It's not completely the fault of the media, but I believe that the media is very biased against us. And I do feel politically the world is against us because the Arabs are much more valuable to them oil-wise.'

Time and again, one finds this unshakable Israeli belief – which is mirrored in the Arab world – that the international community 'is against us'. Does the world outside understand the difficulties and threats faced by Israel, I asked Michal Sudack, an immigrant from Canada, a medical student and young mother living in Beersheba. 'No, I don't think so, I don't think she plays with the media the way she should. I'm not saying that everything Israel does is right and she has to present it that way – like the Lebanon War, the Intifada and all that – but I don't think that Israel puts enough into media and propaganda . . . It's like Israel is the little guy fighting for survival, and yet suddenly it's a country shown doing terrible things to Arab refugees and things like that – I don't think that Israel explains herself there. I think that the Palestinians, whether they do it on purpose or not, manipulate the media very well.'

But why, I wondered, was the Jewish state so poor at public relations when the Jewish lobby in the United States was famous for its success? Michal Sudack's reply backed up my belief that Israel is becoming inextricably linked to the attitudes prevailing in the region. 'I think', she said, 'there's a very large Middle Eastern attitude here. People aren't as sophisticated. The way the Jews manipulate the media in the States, the way everyone does it in the States, everyone's working on a very high level of sophistication. When people come here they just forget it. Take the average person on the street – there's no manners, no sophistication. The sophistication is in the army, in the war machine. That's the thing that Israel does the best, unfortunately – or fortunately, perhaps I should say.'

For the younger generation of Israelis with liberal views about how peace should be achieved the immediate future does not look encouraging. I know of one family which came to Israel many years ago from South Africa; it has now emigrated to Australia. The parents didn't want to raise a young family in a nervous and potentially unstable environment where, for the foreseeable future, Israel would have to remain in a state of aggressive defensiveness towards the rest of the region.

The Professor of Indian Studies quoted at the start of this chapter is another Israeli who is uncertain about the future. He's not sure that he can much longer ignore the trends within Israeli society. 'Israelis have always invested in the "business as usual" mentality. You have to, if you want to live a half normal life here, a certain bloody-minded normalcy.' It's not surprising, he says, that the world at large often fails to understand the mentality of Israel. 'The country began losing ground as her policies became harder, even before the Likud came to power. If you look at the years since, it's a miracle anyone is prepared to talk to us at all. For the last twelve years Israel has had a lunatic foreign policy – except for two years under Labour when it wasn't great either. Here is a country that invaded Lebanon and left us with a useless war, that had to be dragged kicking and screaming to make peace with Egypt, that insists on stealing land in the West Bank, week after week putting up new settlements, and that for two years has been shooting women and children. It's hard to justify any of that . . . This is an Israel that has been taken over by a very destructive force. Self-destructive.'

The Professor's wife, a dance therapist, is no more certain than her husband. 'I ask myself what sort of society this is developing into, because what's happening on a political level is percolating through to all levels of society – there's so much conflict, so much mistrust, so much difficulty between different sectors of the population – and I'm just talking about Israelis, if you include the Arabs, how much more so. It's very frightening. And you ask yourself what sort of society are your children and your grandchildren going to live in.'

The two parents are now agonizing about their future, whether to stay or whether to take up the offer of jobs in the United States. They say they love Israel and feel they have responsibilities to the country. Like most other Israelis, they talk enthusiastically about the positive aspects of bringing up children there – though children have more freedom than in many other parts of the world, they are also faced with the realities of life at an early age and mature young. The lifestyle in Israel is generally healthy – but there is also army duty to be done, and for the eldest son of the Professor and his wife that moment is approaching. His father believes that 'serving in the army now is immoral'. But the son has made it clear that he intends to stay in Israel come what may, and do his army service.

There's another pressure on that family: they, like the majority of Israelis, are Jews, but secular in their lifestyle. Their home is in Jerusalem, and they are unhappy at the way the influence of the ultra-orthodox Jews in the city is growing. Just outside Jerusalem, in a neighbourhood dominated by Jews from Iraq, is the home of a retired paediatrician who came originally from Cape Town in South Africa. Norman Cohen feels no religious pressures in his neighbourhood, but he has watched all the developments in Israel since the formation of the state and before, and in his opinion: 'The religious-secular split in Israel is the biggest problem of all. It's like a time-bomb.'

CHAPTER SIX

———————— •◆• ————————

Religious and secular Israel

R ELIGION itself is a potent force in Israel and throughout the Middle East. It has the power both to unite and divide communities; one united community may turn on another under the banner of religion, one group within a community may take up arms against another. In countries throughout the region fervent religious believers are trying to impose their outlook on the lives of those among whom they live. Israel is no exception.

Religion in the Middle East is inescapable; it is woven into the fabric of every hour that passes and of every action that is taken. Individuals, families, and whole sections in Middle Eastern societies will vary considerably in the degree to which they perform religious rituals or obey religious orders, but religion is a guiding hand for the majority. At times it is visible, at times it is not. And though religion can be a comforter, it can also excite dangerous passions.

The Middle East is the home of three of the major religions in the world: Islam, Judaism and Christianity. It is a region where many early relics of these religions are still to be found; ancient winding streets, caves, tombs, churches, mosques, temples, synagogues – the Middle East is a living museum. Each sacred spot is filled with a cacophony of echoes which have survived the passing of centuries, and eager pilgrims from all three religions come to the Middle East to listen to these voices and to breathe the spiritual air.

Pilgrims to the Middle East have clearly defined objectives, and because the time spent there is limited they usually go away without their spiritual experiences being tainted by the local squabbles, bigotry and hatred. I'm tempted to say that for those in search of a spiritual experience it is almost better to dip in and out of the region like a pilgrim than become immersed in it.

Spending three years of my life in 'The Holy Land', indeed in the city of Jerusalem where three religions jostle and where each one gazes suspiciously on the other two, was always interesting. But seeing the workings of these three religions in close-up was an experience that was often depressing, and certainly not uplifting in any spiritual sense.

Take, for example, the whirlpool of religious emotions on a particular cloudless spring day in 1990. It was Sunday 22 April. For the Jews this was Holocaust Memorial Day; the names of some of the millions of Jews killed during the last World War were being recited in sombre ceremonies all over the country. During the morning sirens had wailed across the Jewish western half of the city, bringing life to a halt for two minutes in memory of the dead. But in Arab East Jerusalem that day ordinary life never even got under way: the underground leadership of the Palestinian uprising had ordered a strike in protest at the unexpected arrival, ten days earlier, of 150 Jewish settlers in the St John's Hospice in the Arab Christian quarter of the Old City. Palestinian fury (both Christian and Muslim) had earlier been directed at the family of an Armenian businessman who was said to have sold the lease to the settlers, thus allowing – for the first time – Jewish penetration into the Christian quarter. (Later that anger was turned on the Israeli government which, it emerged, had contributed money for the purchase of the lease.) In the mean time, that same day extra security precautions were taken in the city as Muslims celebrated the end of the fasting month of Ramadan. Other news items reported more meetings between representatives of the two major political parties in Israel – each struggling to build a new coalition, following the earlier collapse of the government of national unity – and leaders of the small, ultra-orthodox Jewish groups. The latter, holding the balance of power, were seeking to extend their influence in government and on society at large as the price for joining either Labour or Likud.

On that one day in Jerusalem religion, in its different forms and through its different influences (not least on politics and nationalist aspirations), made an unmistakable imprint. But within Israel as a whole, at any time and on any day, religious influence is inescapable, despite the wide variety of views on how, if at all, Judaism is to be practised. The street on the northern edge of Jerusalem where I lived provided a cross-section of those views. A few houses away was a family which was totally secular and liberal in outlook; but on either side of us were families who were observant Jews – they attended the local synagogue regularly, they kept kosher kitchens, and would not drive on the Sabbath. However, both adopted a pragmatic attitude towards the need to observe every single religious rule to the letter, and neither minded if we, as non-Jews, drove our car on the Sabbath and on religious holidays. Other people, ultra-orthodox Jewish families, in streets just half a mile away, did not take such a liberal view and objected very strongly to the Sabbath, as they saw it, being desecrated, whether or not it was by gentiles like me or by fellow Jews. In my three-year stay there was a noticeable increase in the number of streets in Jerusalem which were closed by the police at the beginning of each religious holiday in deference to the wishes of the ultra-orthodox communities. To drive in (or even close to) one of these neighbourhoods on such days would be to risk having your car pelted with stones. One Saturday afternoon shortly after the start of the Palestinian uprising I was driving back from the occupied Gaza Strip, having had my car stoned there by Palestinians. As I drove along the main ring road around the northern outskirts of Jerusalem my car was stoned again – this time by ultra-orthodox Israelis.

The dramatic spread in the influence of religious communities is not confined to Jerusalem, but the phenomenon is more marked there than anywhere. And it tends to be in Jerusalem that the tussles between religious and secular Jews are witnessed. Old-timers say there was once a mutual respect for each other's lifestyles. In 1935 Dov Yinon arrived in Palestine from Poland, escaping anti-Semitism. During the Second World War he was wounded while serving with the British army in Italy. 'We tried to build this country,' he said, 'make it prosperous and give everyone a free choice. In Zionism there was always a nationalist movement which worked in harmony with the religious; they respected the Sabbath and so on. In 1935 Mea Shearim [the area of Jerusalem traditionally dominated by ultra-orthodox Jews] was a small community which everyone respected; they got on with their lives but didn't impose their ways on others.' Now that atmosphere of tolerance has gone.

Chana Cohen drove an ambulance for the British army in Palestine. Her family was religious, but accepted the fact that she married a secular Jew. She and her husband in turn kept a kosher kitchen so that her family could visit them. She remembered driving her ambulance into Mea Shearim, where her grandfather lived. The presence in the ultra-orthodox neighbourhood of a Jewish girl doing a man's job didn't cause a stir. She concludes: 'There was a lot more flexibility then.'

When I arrived in Israel, some months before the start of the Palestinian uprising, the most serious trouble that police in Jerusalem regularly had to deal with was a weekly confrontation between two sections of the Jewish community, the one trying to impose a code of behaviour on the other – religious on secular. The conflict acquired the overly grand title of the War of the Cinemas. Each Friday evening, at the start of the Sabbath, secular Israelis would demonstrate their right, as they saw it, to go to a cinema and watch a film. Ultra-orthodox protesters would try to stop them. The police water-cannon truck would rumble along to whichever cinema had been chosen for that week's protest; there would be some shouting and shoving, occasionally some fighting and stone-throwing; the water cannon would turn its hoses on the crowd; there would be some arrests; and then everyone would go home.

Rather comic encounters of this kind have broken out sporadically since the state of Israel was created, whenever one or other group in society (religious or secular) felt under threat. But emotions run deep on both sides. The wife of a university professor in Jerusalem spoke of her feelings towards religious Jews: 'I feel embarrassed at the fact that I now walk through the streets and when I see a kippa [skull cap] on a man's head I immediately have a reaction of tightening inside my breast. I feel that they [the religious] are rushing together as a throng. And I am more of an individual, somehow, and that thronging of theirs excludes me. That makes me very uncomfortable. There's much more of a need for religious identification because of the terrifying nature of life here, and so people throng together to get a certain comfort. And since I can't embrace what they embrace, it's very divisive.'

Secular Israelis, especially those living in Jerusalem, feel cornered and claustrophobic. Yom Kippur, the Day of Atonement, is a religious holiday like no other in Israel. Observant Jews are required to fast for more than twenty-four hours, from an hour before sunset on the eve, until three stars have appeared in the sky next evening. Streets remain empty: the only vehicles to be seen are the occasional police van or ambulance, and it is not unknown for an ambulance on an emergency mission to be stoned. An Israeli told me about Yom Kippur in 1973; her mother rushed into the room saying: 'There must be trouble – there's traffic!' There was. Another Middle East war had begun.

The fact that the whole population, secular and religious, is expected to observe rituals of abstinence on Yom Kippur and to stay at home is resented by some secular Israelis. One evening, only a few hours after the start of the religious holiday, a secular family from the neighbourhood came to our door. The heavy oppression of both the silence and the imposed mood of religiosity had become too much for them. 'We can't stand it any longer,' one of them said. 'We knew you wouldn't be fasting. Can we come in?'

The next morning, leaving our car parked outside the house, we walked through the empty streets of West Jerusalem (streets which for this one day each year become an extended playground for the children) and walked over into Arab East Jerusalem where life was continuing as normal. On the way we passed the national headquarters of the Israeli police. In one of the watch-towers a guard was on duty as normal, despite the religious holiday, but he was wearing a white prayer-shawl over his blue uniform, and his head and upper body were bobbing as he said his prayers.

In the occupied West Bank, in Jordan, and indeed throughout the Arab world, there is a similar groundswell of acceptance that religious belief and religious rituals should be woven into the fabric of daily life. There are visible signs, such as the clothes people wear. In Arab societies more and more schoolgirls and young women can be seen wearing head scarves and full-length dresses to conform with the degree of modesty expected of them as Muslims. Non-observant Muslims and Christian Arabs are not happy about the trend, but the pressure on them to conform – at least to some extent – is as great as it is in Israel.

For much of the time, even in Jerusalem, the religious-secular conflict remains simmering out of sight. And there is a great deal going on around Israel which could fool a newcomer into thinking that the country is an almost exclusively secular society. One spring afternoon on a semi-deserted beach south of Tel Aviv I noticed the arrival of a fashion photographer (plus sizeable entourage) who had chosen that stretch of Mediterranean shore as a backdrop for his shoot. A model appeared wearing a bikini. As the last adjustments were made to the model's hair and make-up, one male assistant, bare-topped, with his green shirt tied turban-style around his head, set up the camera, while a second, with hair tied into a pig-tail and wearing a green peaked cap, stood ready with a reflector. It was a sight that would not look unusual in any Western country.

At the other extreme, Hebrew and English signs on the walls in the Mea Shearim district of Jerusalem warn women to dress modestly. Bare arms and legs are considered immodest, as they are in, say, Saudi Arabia. The regulations are enforced in Saudi Arabia by the religious police; in Israel's ultra-orthodox Jewish communities by self-styled 'modesty patrols'. A secular Israeli whose house is situated on the fringes of Mea Shearim told me of an incident he witnessed during which two female tourists wearing shorts were confronted and chased away by two ultra-orthodox men even before they'd entered the neighbourhood. This infuriated the secular witness. As far as he was concerned he was prepared to let the ultra-orthodox live by their own rules within their neighbourhood, but here was another sign of the 'blacks' (as he and other secular Israelis disparagingly call them because of their black coats and hats) expanding their boundaries.

This is the dilemma faced by all Middle Eastern countries. How is the balance to be struck between religious and secular life? Can the two be compartmentalized? In Iran, the Shah wanted to eradicate the distinction by making his country broadly secular in outlook and by turning to the West as his model. The reaction pushed the country in exactly the opposite direction. In most other Middle Eastern countries, Islamic pressure has forced changes in regulations (like the banning of the sale of alcohol in public places in Egypt, for example). Similar pressures are at work within Israel. So it is that rabbis in Jerusalem have banned belly-dancing at kosher places of entertainment, arguing that the performances of what the rabbis describe as 'the scantily clad dancers' are immoral. This, despite the fact that belly-dancing is an integral part of the culture of Jews from Oriental countries and is a popular form of entertainment at weddings and other religious celebrations. (For similar reasons, public performances of belly-dancing in Arab countries are becoming rare, as night-clubs in Egypt and elsewhere come under pressure from Islam.) In June 1990 the High Court in Jerusalem ruled that the rabbinate's ban on belly-dancing was illegal. But rabbis were seeking other ways of stopping the performances.

Tel Aviv and Jerusalem are separate worlds. While almost all visible life has evaporated from the streets of Jerusalem by the time the Shabbat (Sabbath) siren dolefully announces the start of the holy day on Friday evening, in Tel Aviv a city is coming to life and relishing the prospect of a lively night ahead. Each year, too, there is the Miss Israel contest to look forward to. 'Ten thousand people', the newspaper report of one such event began:

> the would-be trendy wearing Tel Aviv black and the common folk wearing whatever common folk wear filled the Yad Eliahu stadium to see which of 20 beauties would be Israel's candidate at the Miss Universe pageant in April in Los Angeles. The orchestra, which had a weakness for the theme from Dynasty, was all in white, as was emcee [sic] Dudu Topaz, as was the stage, which looked like a huge styrofoam wedding cake. Under flashing coloured lights the contestants circled the stage in peasant dresses, evening gowns and bathing suits. No. 8, Meirav Razon, kept tugging at the seat of her leopard-skin suit, aware that she was showing a bit too much buttock . . .

If the *status quo* were maintained in this compartmentalized way, then probably most secular Israelis would be happy. But it is not. Religious rulings impinge on many aspects of life. The opening of a luxury hotel in Jerusalem had to be delayed while all the locks were changed on the doors. The electronic 'key-card' system, which is in use increasingly throughout the world, had been installed, but the rabbinate refused the hotel its kosher certificate because the use of the card involves creating an electric spark, which – under Halacha, religious law – is not allowed on the Sabbath. So all the electronic locks had to be removed and mechanical key-locks installed in their place before the hotel was allowed to open. In another example of religious involvement in secular affairs, a much-needed multi-million-pound investment offered by an American electronic components company for the development town of Karmiel in Galilee in northern Israel was thrown into doubt because of difficulties securing permits to allow the plant to operate on the Sabbath. Without such an agreement the American company was not prepared to invest the money, and 1700 potential jobs would have been lost.

Just as Islamic pressures in Jordan have forced that country's national airline to stop serving alcohol to passengers, so pressures from ultra-orthodox Jewish groups have forced the national airline of Israel, El Al, to stop all flights on the Sabbath and religious holidays. The grounding of its fleet for twenty-four hours each week is, not surprisingly, a major inconvenience, not to mention financial burden, for El Al. Regulations of this kind infuriate secular Israelis not only because they are a sign of the power that religious groups can wield within the political system and within society at large, but also because of what they see as the underlying hypocrisy of the legislation. For just as a Muslim who feels strongly enough that he wants to drink a glass of wine with his meal while flying to London will simply choose an airline other than Royal Jordanian, so a Jew who wants to travel on the Sabbath will choose an airline other than El Al. A columnist in the *Jerusalem Post* argued the point in the following way:

> The sin of the unbeliever is not only the act of travelling, it is the desire to travel. Halting El Al flights will not undo this transgression. Orthodox politicians enforcing this ban, regardless of passengers' wishes, are guilty of deception. They pretend the law is being obeyed when it isn't. Religious people who feel good at the weekly standstill confuse animate people with inanimate objects. The only thing immobilized is the inanimate plane; the conduct of the Jews is unaffected.

But changing the conduct of Jews is exactly the aim of the orthodox groups. And they have found the perfect vehicle for their endeavour: the Israeli political system. In recent years general elections have seen the two major parties, Labour and Likud, winning about an equal share of seats in the Knesset. So each party has needed to 'buy' the support of the smaller far-left, far-right, or religious groups to command a majority. This has given the religious parties the opportunity to exercise an influence which far exceeds their numerical strength inside the Knesset or their public support outside it.

Among the Jewish people of Israel about twenty per cent of the population comes under the category of being 'religious', to the extent that they keep kosher homes (with, for example, strict separation, in both the preparation and eating, between meat and dairy products), attend synagogues and observe the Sabbath. But they would not necessarily vote for religious parties. In addition to this twenty per cent, another ten per cent or so are ultra-orthodox. For them, the Torah and the command- ments contained in it represent the lifestyle to strive for.

For the orthodox Jew, as much as for the pious Muslim, religion is inseparable from daily life, but within orthodox communities of both

Jews and Muslims there are divisions, based on differing interpretations, on social background, or on the influence of individual personalities. Variations found among the Jewish ultra-orthodox community remain obscure and difficult to comprehend for many Israelis – how much more so, then, for an outsider?' Among them one finds Ha'Eda Haharedit (the community of the 'Haredi' or God-fearing), made up of an estimated 7,000 families who were established in Jerusalem before the creation of the state of Israel. They are opposed to and do not recognize the state of Israel, and as a result do not take part in local or national politics. Their everyday language is Yiddish, because they believe that it is heresy to speak Hebrew, the language of the Torah, until the coming of the Messiah.

Other members of the ultra-orthodox community, while not being happy at the existence of what they regard as a secular Jewish state (i.e. one which isn't following the commandments of the Torah to the letter), are prepared to make accommodation with it. (The label Haredi (God-fearing) is commonly attached by Israelis to all members of the ultra-orthodox community, not just to members of Ha'Eda Haharedit.) Agudat Israel is the oldest of the ultra-orthodox parties, and served as an umbrella group for members of the ultra-orthodox community before and after the creation of the state of Israel when there were two other major groups within society: the secular Zionists and the religious Zionists. Agudat Israel was anti-Zionist for many years and even today different members of it define their Zionism in different ways.

Recent years have seen deep-rooted, 200-year-old historical splits within the ultra-orthodox community re-emerge in Israel, highlighting the difference between the scholarly, formalistic approach to Judaism of the Jews of Lithuania and the less rigid and less intellectual attitude of the Hassidic Jews from Poland and Eastern Europe. Agudat Israel remains the party representing the Hassidic Jews, while the Lithuanian strain has broken away in the form of a party called Degel Hatorah (flag of the Torah). A third split has come with the appearance of Shas, a party formed by and on behalf of ultra-orthodox Jews from Oriental countries, with the encouragement and patronage of the Lithuanian strain. Under the banner of Agudat Israel can also be found the Habad movement, the leader of which is known as the Rabbi of Lubavitch. While he lives in New York and has never visited Israel, he has been able to exert an enormous amount of influence over political developments in the Jewish state.

During the search for a new government, after the collapse of the Labour-Likud coalition of national unity in the first half of 1990, the influence of elderly rabbis who are critical of the existence of Israel could be clearly felt on the political stage. At one point the Labour leader, Mr Peres, thought he had sufficient support, with the backing of Agudat Israel, to form a government. At the very last minute, though, on the advice of the elderly Rabbi of Lubavitch, Menachem Schneerson, two Aguda Knesset members deserted Labour, and Mr Peres failed to form a government. The Rabbi's intervention exasperated and angered, not surprisingly, Labour and its left-wing supporters. Yossi Sarid of the Citizens Rights Movement said it was 'a most frightening fact that an old Jew, nearly ninety, sitting in Brooklyn is dictating what happens in Israel – if this isn't crazy, I don't know what is.'

At an earlier stage during the same period the eventual outcome of the efforts to form a new government seemed to rest in the hands of a nonagenarian rabbi, Eliezer Schach, the leader of Degel Hatorah. It was announced that on a particular Monday night, in front of a large crowd of his supporters in a basketball stadium in Tel Aviv (where the 'Miss Israel' contest is held), he would declare which way his party would tilt the balance. The evening came, and with the hall packed, not just with his supporters but also with journalists (male only) and cameramen, and with the whole event being shown live on Israel Television, all eyes were on the frail, stooped figure in front of the microphones, with his black hat, black-rimmed glasses and thick white beard. He spoke at times in Hebrew, at other times in Yiddish. A clear-cut endorsement of one or other party it most certainly was not: rather it was an address which showed how wide the chasm is between ultra-orthodox and secular Israel. The rabbi took to task both Labour and Likud, but he reserved his harshest judgement for the former. Parties on the left, he said, had been responsible for the education which had alienated a whole generation from Judaism. The kibbutz movement, he went on, 'don't know about the Sabbath. They don't know about the mikveh (ritual bath) . . . One told me he'd never been to a synagogue . . . can you call people like this Jews?'

Labour leaders were angry and indignant. And even for an outsider it was hard to believe that the future of Israel, a regional super-power, a state with nuclear capability and the skill to put a satellite into space, was in the hands of such men. The spirit of what Rabbi Schach said seemed similar to the kind of pronouncements heard during Friday prayers in Tehran, in Cairo or in Algiers, by religious men who seem trapped in a former century. 'The modern secular world has failed you; you've lost your way. Religion in its purest, most fundamental form is your only salvation.' This is the message of Middle Eastern religious fundamentalism. One daily newspaper in Israel commented that the power of the ultra-orthodox now meant that while Eastern European countries 'were throwing off the yoke of autocracy, we are in the throes of political regression'. But the daily newspaper published by Degel Hatorah, *Yated Ne'eman*, disagreed: 'Rabbi Schach spelled out the central plan of Degel Hatorah: in order for the Jewish people to survive they must remain a *Jewish* nation.'

Secular Israelis – not least the women – believe that there is already too much religious coercion within society. There is no civil marriage, for example. And just as the rabbi has to be involved when a Jewish couple want to get married, so too it is the religious court which decides when one or other of them wants a divorce. Under Jewish law, though, both partners have to agree in order that a divorce can be granted. Women say that if there's disagreement, then the rabbi invariably takes the side of the man. As a result, a woman is liable to find herself in an unenviable position: abandoned by her husband, yet unable to get a divorce because the rabbis won't allow it. What makes matters worse, women say, is that while a married man can go off and live with (or on rare occasions even marry) another woman – and have children – without society turning a hair, it's quite a different matter for an abandoned wife. To live with another man while she is formally married is to be branded an adulteress, and any children born of that liaison will have a diminished religious and legal status when they come to marry.

Those members of the religious communities who take part in the political process in Israel do so, they say, in order both to encourage legislation for greater observance of Halacha (religious law) and to stake a claim for a more equitable distribution of the state budget. They accuse successive governments of providing insufficient funds for housing and schools in religious neighbourhoods. 'In secular families,' Rabbi Avraham Verdiger of Agudat Israel said, 'you have one child and one dog; in religious families there are ten children.' Therefore, it is argued, there should be an increase in funding commensurate with the increase in the population.

The big difference in the birth-rate between secular and orthodox families is one of the reasons cited by Rabbi Menachem Porush of Agudat Israel for his optimism that the religious community will continue to expand, and that the secular-religious balance will change in favour of the religious. But there are other reasons as well: 'Religious people are not running away from Israel. Religious people look upon Israel as the holy land, the land of the Bible. And the Bible promised the Jewish people: this is your land. . . . Secular elements are running away to America and other places.'

Rabbi Emanuel Feldman of Atlanta in Georgia, USA, wrote in the *Jerusalem Post* while on sabbatical in Israel:

> Those supposedly raised on a pure Zionist diet abandon Israel for the lure of the West, while those raised on Torah and mitzvot find it easy to leave behind the luxurious life of the West for a less comfortable existence in Israel . . . Admittedly, the Haredim make many Israelis uncomfortable. The reality of their numbers, discipline and strength . . . engenders anger and fear. At the very least, it is difficult to identify with black hats, kapottes and long beards, and with attitudes that seem unaccommodating to Western ways . . . They have large families, which may horrify their sophisticated Israeli brethren (who fashion-ably have one of the world's lowest birth-rates); but they are the only ones matching the Arab population explosion, which threatens to engulf Israel within a generation.

Observations of this kind strike a chord in me. For this is the language, the raw, unambiguous and inflexible language, of Middle Eastern fundamentalism. And the experience of other countries of the region has shown that when times are hard, or when people are confused or depressed by what is going on around them, they turn back to religion. The reawakening of interest in religion is not necessarily the same as fundamentalism, but in that climate fundamentalism thrives. It is happening in just about every Arab country, and, with comparable certainty, orthodox Jews in Israel are convinced that there is a tide moving in their direction and away from the secular path.

Avraham Greenbaum studies and writes books in a small flat in Mea Shearim which you reach by climbing up a scruffy flight of stairs from the street. He is quietly spoken; he wears a black cap from which ringlets of fair hair fall, and a fair beard flows down from his pale face. Avraham Greenbaum used to be a radio producer in London; now he has found contentment in Mea Shearim, an area which he says has 'a ring of tremendous antiquity'. I asked him about the unexpected success of the religious parties at the general election in November 1988. 'I would like to think', he replied, 'that more people are beginning to question the values with which they were brought up in the early years of the state, and see that secular Zionism doesn't really answer your existential questions about "What should I do with my life, how do I answer those cosmic questions?" As people awaken to that I'd like to think that people become more aware of their religious heritage.' A renewed interest among young Israelis in the study of Jewish mysticism is also ascribed to this trend.

In the view of Avraham Greenbaum Israel will remain in what he calls 'a state of spiritual exile' until the time when the Torah directs the lives of everyone in the country. He is not in favour of introducing legislation. 'Laws won't change people's consciousness or their hearts. I personally would not spend my time campaigning for legislation. You can achieve more by talking directly to people's hearts and showing that to observe the Torah is actually such a beautiful way of life that if you're doing it properly people will just be drawn in after you. Because they'll see that you're such a fulfilled person.'

The attraction of a clear and certain statement like this is obvious. In a similar way the Muslims declare with disarming confidence and simplicity: 'There is no God but Allah.' A Jewish state following the Torah and becoming 'a light unto the nations'; an Islamic state throughout the Middle East – for true believers this is heady stuff. In Israel as in Arab countries, there is a sizeable proportion of the population who are steeped in either Jewish or Islamic culture and tradition (and may indeed be practising Jews, Muslims or Christians), but who would not welcome such far-reaching developments. What is absolutely clear, though, is that the appeal of such fundamentalist approaches to religion in the Middle East is growing.

Moshe Schlass, an artist and follower of the ultra-orthodox Habad movement living in the Old City of Jerusalem, declares: 'People come to Israel from countries which aren't Jewish, where their attitude about their identity is played down so as not to rub people up the wrong way. So the whole concept of confronting your roots is not a reality. A lot of people come from backgrounds that are assimilated, or from religious backgrounds where they were religious only because their parents were, and it had no meaning for them. As soon as they had the chance to throw off the yoke, they did. But as you'll find out, there's been a great reawakening, myself included, in the revival of Jewish identity. So what you see here is a process, it won't be here very long . . . In the time to come, and very shortly, the prophecies will be fulfilled. Israel will become a theocracy. The ruler will be from the roots of King David, and it will be according to God's will. And not only will Israel be fine, but the whole world will be fine.'

Until such time as Israel is a 'theocracy' or the Middle East is an Islamic state the reality is very different. Secular outlooks, materialism and indifference are not going to disappear overnight. National frontiers may become irrelevant in the future when nationalistic aspirations are swept aside by a tidal wave of religious euphoria, but that day is still nowhere in sight. The Jewish state, imperfect though it might be in the eyes of the ultra-orthodox community, exists because Jews have been prepared to fight for it. A section of the ultra-orthodox community living in Mea Shearim takes no part in Israeli life, while making use of the services provided by the state. In addition, yeshiva students (those studying the Torah in religious seminaries) are not required to serve the three-year period in the army followed by annual reserve duty which is compulsory for every other Israeli male. This tradition of exemption began immediately after the creation of Israel. Rabbis at that time argued that the yeshiva community in Europe had been so decimated that it was essential to build up a new one in the Jewish state, and the first Prime Minister of Israel, David Ben-Gurion, agreed to grant exemption to several hundred religious students. Over the years that number has crept up to something like 18,000 Israelis at any one time having their military service 'deferred' (as it is formally termed). Secular females do two years of compulsory army service. Most observant females receive exemption.

In a small country which feels under threat and where enormous value is put on the army and the national duty of serving in it, 18,000 is a very large number – especially given that by May 1990 16,951 Israeli soldiers had died in the defence of the Jewish state. The exemption granted to the religious community is the source of very deep resentment among many Israelis, secular and religious alike. The need for Torah scholarship is recognized; but the feeling is that the system is being abused by Israelis who want to avoid the army. 'There's nothing wrong with there being, for example, a handful of scholars in Britain devoted to the study of Chaucer,' a retired Israeli army general commented to me once, 'but would you really need 18,000 of them?' After the speech by Rabbi Schach mentioned earlier in this chapter, accusing the left in Israel of alienating Jews from religion, Yossi Sarid, a Knesset member representing the Citizens Rights Movement, wondered if there was someone in Israel 'who in the next war – God forbid – will be willing to give up the sons of the Labour movement and the kibbutz and send the yeshiva boys'. And in a reference to suggestions that Jews did not do enough to resist the Nazi drive to exterminate them during the Second World War, Yossi Sarid continued: 'The security doctrine of Rabbi Schach was tried by the Jewish people several times in the past – and the last time was in the Holocaust.'

Within Israel there has always been a section of society which was both religious and Zionist. When the state of Israel was created, religious Zionists faced a dilemma. This was without doubt 'the ingathering of the exiles' as promised by God, for which Jews had prayed for centuries. But the state itself was both created by and was being run by secular Jews. Dr Daniel Tropper, the founder and director of the Gesher Foundation for understanding between the secular and observant communities, explained in an article in the *Jerusalem Post* that while the ultra-orthodox:

> chose the route of rejection and challenged the legitimacy of the state . . . . the religious Zionists chose a completely different route, one of accommodation. The secular-Jewish state, it allowed, is indeed not what we anticipated, but it is, nevertheless, a miraculous gift of God. It has some weaknesses, some blatant and religiously repugnant. Our mission, however, is not to make its historic task more difficult but to participate in its growth and help it move to higher spiritual heights.

Religious Zionism occupies the middle ground in a country which is becoming polarized between left and right, between liberal secularism and ultra-nationalist Zionism. Dr Tropper believes that 'the pursuit of the national good has been supplanted by the quest for personal goods. Various political and economic developments have combined with this social process to cause an estrangement of the intellectual élite of Israeli society from everything collective: religion, Jewishness and nationalism. The Israeli intelligentsia of today looks with suspicion on all three, even nationalism.' The result, Dr Tropper continues, is that 'even the Haredi community, though more limited in intellectual breadth and resented for not sharing the burden of defence, seems more rational to the secularists because its non-nationalistic orientation has fostered an intensely personalized religion which is far more comprehensible to the modern Israeli. Religious Zionism is being outflanked on all sides and is being reduced to a trivial anachronism.'

In the November 1988 general election campaign a new party called Meimad tried to reclaim some of the middle ground by attracting religious Jews who had liberal views on the question of peace with the Arabs and the future of the Occupied Territories. In the election itself, ultra-orthodox parties did surprisingly well; Meimad failed to win a seat. There may have been faults in the way Meimad presented its views and handled its campaign, but the result, in the view of Itzhak Galnoor, Professor of Political Science at the Hebrew University, contained a clear message: "The religious camp as we knew it in the pre-state period and up to the Six Day War is no more. Nothing testifies more to this assertion than does the painful failure of Meimad, the new moderate religious party headed by Rabbi Yehuda Amital. Meimad received less than 16,000 votes . . . Meimad tried to reach out to observant and traditional Jews who resent the stigma of extremism branded on them by both Gush Emunim and Habad. Meimad was willing to think about territorial compromise, and it emphasized Jewish education rather than coercive religious legislation. But moderate religion has been on the decline in Israel since 1967.'

Moderate religion has been on the decline throughout the Middle East for some years. Aside from the obvious example of Iran, one can point to the general self-assertion of Islamic fundamentalist groups from North Africa to the Gulf. In some countries these groups work openly within the system, as in Jordan; in others they operate underground, as in Syria or Iraq.

This trend is either a blessing or a curse, depending on your point of view. What seems clear, though, is that the unmistakable drift towards fundamentalist religion in the Middle East is going to make the resolution of the Arab-Israeli conflict more difficult. The two sides may start speaking the same kind of language, but it is generally not the language of compromise and tolerance, since in both Israel and the Arab world religious fundamentalism is also a vehicle for nationalism. Jerusalem is the 'capital' of three religions. Two of them (Judaism and Islam) claim it in the name of nations as well. The three years which I spent in Jerusalem witnessed barriers of religious and national hatred being built more often than being dismantled.

Rabbi Mordechai Sheinberger is a distinguished scholar of cabbalism – Jewish mysticism – living in the Jewish quarter of the Old City of Jerusalem. He is a man of great presence which is transmitted not by bluster or physical stature, but by calmness. He has strong, light-blue eyes, pale delicate hands, and a silver-grey beard. In speaking about the religious–secular divide in Israel he (like all religious Jews I met) was certain that the day would come when all Jews would live according to the Torah. 'Beyond this,' he continued, 'there is also an emotional side to it all. Jews have been chased for thousands of years, they've never had a country. They experienced the Holocaust. Now it's time for them to have a place where they can live quietly and in peace. It's really important for the Jews to have a country where they can live peacefully and confidently, and not feel that there's hatred coming from within them, that's stopping them living that way. Because there's so much hatred coming from the Arabs, and I don't believe it's going to change. It's impossible for us to live in the same country as the Arabs because it just doesn't allow the Jews to live in the way they should finally be allowed to live after all these thousands of years.' Was he suggesting that the Arabs should be kicked out? 'They have to be given a place which is theirs and is separate from us.'

The focus of religious controversy in Jerusalem between Jews and Muslims (and because of the overlap between religion and nationalism the site is equally the subject of intense nationalistic controversy) is Mount Moriah, the raised ground at the eastern end of the Old City. Jews call it the Temple Mount and Muslims call it the Haram al-Sharif (the Noble Sanctuary). Today it is the site of the best-known and most beautiful feature of the Jerusalem skyline, the Dome of the Rock: under its distinctive gold-leafed dome and elaborate mosaics lies the rock on which Abraham is believed to have been prepared to sacrifice his son Isaac. Just to the south stands the Aqsa mosque, with its smaller black dome, revered by Muslims as the spot where the Prophet Muhammad made his night ascension to heaven. The problems arise from the fact that the Haram al-Sharif was constructed on the site of the first and second Jewish temples. The first was destroyed in 587 BC, the second in AD 70. The fifty-foot-high Western wall of the second temple is all that remains, and is as much the spiritual focus for every Jew as Mecca is for Muslims. When the Israeli army captured the old city of Jerusalem in the 1967 War, the Haram al-Sharif was left in the hands of the Muslim authorities, who allow individual Jews to visit but not pray in the area. The orthodox rabbinate (the established religious hierarchy in Israel) says that no Jews should go on to the Temple Mount for fear of desecrating the 'Holy of Holies' of the second temple buried somewhere beneath the surface.

This state of affairs, accepted by Jewish and Muslim leaders, is a source of irritation to a good number of Israelis. Some fanatics believe that Israel should take over the Temple Mount and build the third Jewish temple there; plans have been drawn up for such a temple, scale models have been built, and materials gathered for the interior. Jewish extremists have tried on five occasions since 1967 to blow up the Aqsa mosque or Dome of the Rock. A group called the Temple Mount Faithful frequently clashes with police while trying to enter the mosque area to pray. In October 1989 the group announced that it was going to lay a cornerstone for the new Jewish temple. Gershon Salomon, leader of the 'Faithful', and a small group of followers arrived for the ceremony, but the police would not allow the lorry carrying the huge stone into the area, fearing the spread of anti-Israeli demonstrations which had already broken out in Arab East Jerusalem. This did not stop Gershon Salomon picking up his megaphone and declaring that: 'We have started a process . . . With this act we close an historic circle which started one thousand nine hundred and nineteen years ago, when the temple, Jerusalem and the state of Israel [sic] were destroyed by the enemy . . . Not long [from now] this process will put an end to the Arab presence on the Temple Mount which is a memory of Arab colonialism and Arab imperialism before thirteen hundred years when they came to the Temple Mount, to Jerusalem, to the country of Israel.'

This is the voice of the extremist fringe, but echoes of the intolerance implicit in the words are depressingly common these days among both Israelis and Arabs (Christians and Muslims). The balance between the competing religions and sects in Jerusalem is delicate, as the uproar which followed the arrival of Jewish settlers in the Christian quarter of the Old City in the spring of 1990 showed. And consider the following observation by an inhabitant (of American origin) of the Jewish Quarter: 'There should be no Arabs on the Temple Mount. They have their holy sites, they have their place in Mecca. They can have mosques wherever they want, making noise until five o'clock in the morning, shooting off those loudspeakers and disturbing everyone's sleep. That's democratic. That's very nice. If we Jews would do such a thing we'd get into a lot of trouble, get a ticket for having a party after eleven o'clock. You're having a good time at a bar mitzvah or a wedding – the cops come and tell you to be quiet. These things from the mosques go off at two-thirty in the morning, or in the middle of prayers at the Wall. But, oh yes, that's democratic, that's fine.'

In his house in Mea Shearim Avraham Greenbaum takes a calmer and more charitable view of the gulf between Jews and Muslims. His perspective is ultra-orthodox, but shorn of ultra-nationalist undertones. 'I think, given that many of the Arabs are more traditionalist, it probably irks them to see the Jews living such a very secular life here. Especially an Arab who is religious. He sees what the Jew does as an affront to religion in two respects – as an affront to the standards which Islam holds to in terms of modesty of dress by women, restraint in the way you eat, etc; and an affront in terms of Islam's view of what the Jew is supposed to be.'

So much for the outside view; but what about the view from the inside – who exactly is a Jew? As a non-Jew I would not presume to attempt an answer – thus my surprise when this very question became an explosive political issue after the November 1988 elections. Some members of the religious parties, as part of their terms for agreeing to join either Labour or Likud to form a new coalition, wanted legislation to amend the Law of Return, the most fundamental of all the laws in Israel. This gives every Jew the right to settle in Israel and become an Israeli citizen. But who is a Jew? He or she, according to the Law of Return, is either someone born of a Jewish mother, or else a convert. Rabbis who want a change in the law do not recognize conversions to Judaism carried out by rabbis of the Conservative and Reform movements because the ceremonies have not been performed according to religious law – Halacha. Therefore, their argument goes, those converts should not have the automatic right to settle in Israel, and an amendment to this effect should be made to the Law of Return. Other orthodox and ultra-orthodox leaders in Israel hold that there is no need to amend the law, because Reform and Conservative rabbis are not allowed to register marriages, perform ceremonies like weddings or grant divorces. Or, to be more precise, such ceremonies when conducted by them are not recognized by the state, therefore they have no status. Any Jew coming to Israel – from whatever Jewish background – has no choice but to conform to the practices of orthodox Judaism on a number of key matters affecting his life.

'Who is a Jew?' is an emotive and explosive issue within the Jewish community as a whole. And little wonder. If such a change to the Law of Return were ever introduced, then overnight many thousands of Jews who had been converted by Conservative and Reform rabbis would find that they no longer had the right to become Israelis. This would cause deep offence in the United States where the vast majority of Jews are followers of Conservative and Reform Judaism. It is perhaps little wonder that these questions about the fundamental roots of religion are being asked in the Middle East, in a region which contains so many intolerant voices – like those calling for the destruction of the Haram al-Sharif in order to cement the foundation of the 'one thousand nine hundred and nineteen year old Jewish state'; or like those others demanding the destruction of the modern Zionist state to make way for the creation of an Islamic fundamentalist-dominated Middle East.

Israel today poses questions tinged with the intolerant rhetoric of the Middle East, as well as many other questions about the future, for those Jews who are planning to come to the country; and for those who are wondering whether or not to stay.

CHAPTER SEVEN

Comings and goings

Soon after nightfall we could get a dialling tone again. A neighbour had come round during the afternoon to see if our phone was working because hers didn't appear to be. But with all the authority of a visiting foreigner I was able to assure her that we had the same problem, and that it was nothing to worry about. Neither of us had been cut off either deliberately or accidentally; it was just that the whole telephone system was overloaded with Israelis calling up to greet their friends and relatives at home and abroad. I remembered the same thing happening on the two previous eves of the Jewish New Year that I had experienced. It is on Jewish holidays above all, I was told, that Jews sense their Diaspora (dispersion) most keenly.

The dream of most Israelis is that one day the prayer for 'the ingathering of the exiles' will be fulfilled. But it's a dream that seems unlikely to be turned into reality in even the distant future. Until such a time, Israelis will be located within a Middle Eastern scene which is characterized by wandering tribes – groups and individuals heading off in search, perhaps of work, of fortune, of family reunification, or spiritual satisfaction. Tales of Middle Eastern migration may conjure up images of camel trains silhouetted against the setting desert sun, but the real picture in the last quarter of the twentieth century is of the jostling and shoving at airport departure halls in, say, Cairo, Jeddah or Baghdad: and of edgy and irritable families crowding round boarding gates in New York or London for flights to Tel Aviv. The true images are of families sprawled over airport seating, surrounded by suitcases, parcels, stereo radio-cassette players, and boxes of disposable nappies, of elderly faces furrowed by the agony of farewells, and of the wide cabins of long-distance jets crammed with uprooted humanity.

The pattern of migration within the Arab world has been one of people either leaving the region in search of employment in the developed world – especially in Europe or the United States; or leaving big centres of population, like Egypt, for areas of economic growth in the Middle East – especially oil-rich Gulf states. Since the creation of the state of Israel in 1948, Palestinians have been a rich ingredient in the fluid of Arab migration.

Israel itself is, by definition, a category apart. Migration within the region remains an impossibility, and throughout the century the whole emphasis of Zionism had been on bringing Jews to that part of the land in the Middle East which the world at large was eventually to accept as the modern state of Israel. Since then there has been constant movement between Israel and the Jewish communities outside, not least those in the United States. My assumption was that this to-ing and fro-ing was mainly tourism and family visits, disguising an underlying trend which saw Jews from the United States and elsewhere in the world gradually (and at a pace which was regarded by Israelis as depressingly and frustratingly slow) putting down roots in the Jewish state. Thus I was shocked to hear, even as the prayers for the 'ingathering of the exiles' continue to be said, that the migration of Israelis is a two-way traffic of some considerable volume. There are, according to reliable estimates, more than half a million Israelis now living in the United States and Canada. Israelis, that is – not North American Jews.

To migrate to Israel is to 'make aliyah' – aliyah being the Hebrew word for ascent. To quote the *Political Dictionary of the State of Israel* (edited by Susan Hattis Rolef and published in Jerusalem by Keter), aliyah 'expresses the ideological motive – both religious and Zionist – for Jewish migration to Eretz Israel (the Land of Israel), and distinguishes it from other migrant movements motivated by over-population, the discovery of new lands, the search for riches, etc. It expresses the Jewish striving to return to the land of the forefathers, the Holy Land, and the termination of the punishment of exile,' which is reflected in prayers said by observant Jews three times each day. Apart from the above reasons, though, in most instances the movement of Jews to Israel reflected insecurity and persecution as much as ideology.

If the arrival in Israel is regarded as a triumphant 'ascent', then it follows that the departure must be a 'descent', with all its shameful and negative connotations. And so it is. In Hebrew the word is 'yeridah', but there is no entry for it in the *Political Dictionary*. It is clearly not a comfortable subject, and is swept under the carpet as much as possible. Shmuel Lahis, a former head of the Jewish Agency (one of the bodies encouraging migration to Israel) is determined that this state of affairs should change, and now heads a group called Citizens for the Prevention of Emigration. Towards the middle of 1990 he estimated that there were 650,000 Israelis living in North America alone, and he took issue with official figures which try to minimize the extent of yeridah. The Statistical Bureau, he claims, 'is playing a shameful game by not giving the correct figure'. The differences arise over the definition of a 'yored', an *émigré*. Shmuel Lahis says the United Nations definition is: a person who has lived out of his country for at least one year. He believes that two years is a more realistic figure; the Israeli government says that a citizen can be defined as an *émigré* only when he has been away for four years. What is beyond dispute, though, is that hundreds of thousands of Israelis are living abroad, and that about 20,000 are leaving each year. This meant that, until the recent surge in the numbers of Jews arriving from the Soviet Union, there has at times been a net loss from Israel's point of view.

You get a sense of this fluidity by talking to Israelis as much as by talking to Arabs. It seems, in the Middle East, that once the subject comes round to families, you inevitably hear how one son is studying in Europe or how one daughter or sister is married and living in New York or California. Norman Cohen realizes how lucky he is to be an exception to this rule. He came to Palestine in the 1940s from South Africa, and is a paediatrician, now retired. He met his wife Chana when he went to Hebrew lessons and she was the teacher. 'We count our blessings,' he said, 'because our three children and all our grandchildren are here in Israel . . . it's like living in a pressure-cooker here and lots of young people go away after the army.' Chana continued: 'If I count my friends, every family has at least one child out of the country. It's sad.'

It is true that, after three years in the army straight after leaving school (or two years, in the case of young women), many Israelis leave the country. Some just want to travel for a few months, to see the world and to get the army experience out of their system, before coming back to Israel to work or study; but others, finding when they have finished with the army that there are no jobs and that they have no prospect of setting up their own homes, go in search of work overseas. Shmuel Lahis says his concern is that once they have gone there is very little hope of bringing them back, and Israel is, therefore, losing its most valuable asset: people. What's needed, he believes, is financial encouragement to help these young people get on their feet and overcome frustration at the lack of opportunities when they are discharged from the army. Once they have gone abroad (and with so many family links with the Jewish community around the world, this is no great problem), they are prepared to do any kind of work simply to make a living. 'After three or four years,' Shmuel Lahis goes on, 'many are longing to come back to Israel. But this is our real tragedy.' He says Israelis living abroad feel a sense of guilt for having left and want to be able to justify their actions by showing that they've improved their position while away. And they'll have no chance of coming back with their heads held high if they know there are no jobs to come to and no apartments which they can afford.

The phenomenon is not just confined to youngsters. A Hebrew-language newspaper at the end of 1989 reported that emigrants over the past year had included 'financially well-established businessmen and professionals, not just youths or jobless people seeking fortunes elsewhere. They are packing full households and moving their families and businesses to, in particular, the United States, Canada, Australia and Britain.'

The need to make a living is clearly a major reason why Israelis leave the country. But as often as not, in my experience, chance and circumstances also play a role in these decisions. The artist Anita Kushner was born and raised in Philadelphia in the United States in a totally secular family. 'As a child I didn't even know that Shabbat existed, that Saturday was sacred to the Jews at all. The few Yiddish words I knew were what my friends the Adams – a real "WASP" family – taught me. And they'd picked up those words from living in New York.' Years later, as an adult in 1968, Anita Kushner decided to move to Israel. How did she decide? 'I was sitting in the bath tub having a bath – I was married – and I said to my husband (now my ex-husband): "Let's go to Israel." Just out of the clear blue sky. He wasn't at all interested.' But even at that stage Anita Kushner said she 'had the wierdest idea of Israel. If I'd been brought up a Christian I'd have known more. I thought that if they caught an adulterer or adulteress they'd stone them in the streets. I didn't know what to expect.'

The patterns of migration in the Middle East are rich and complicated, and are often stained by bitterness and misunderstanding. I know of a family who came to Israel as dedicated Zionists in the 1950s. They later returned to Canada, disillusioned at the way Israel was developing. One of their daughters, who was born in the United States while her father was attached to a university there and who in adulthood has become very religious, is now living in Israel, troubled and depressed by the way that her parents have turned their backs on the country. The daughter worked off some of her feelings by putting them in a letter to her father in Canada. And he responded to them. This correspondence between daughter and father reveals the poignant and complex relationship between generations and between the different images that Jews (even within the same family) have about the kind of Israel they want to see when they 'make aliyah'. Here is part of what the daughter wrote to her father in Canada:

My grandparents are buried on a hillside in Jerusalem, overlooking the road to Tel Aviv. For a year and a half I have not visited their graves. Nor, I'm certain, has anyone else, for I am the only one – me here, alone in Jerusalem – living out their dream.

My grandfather died when I was three years old. I have no memories of him, yet my head is full of stories. He was a Talmud chacham [a brilliant scholar of the Torah], and a man with vision, leaving his native Russia at the age of seventeen to explore the wild Canadian north, inspired by poetry and legends he had read. He wrote about that barren, snowy land in biblical Hebrew, tales published in a book after which my youngest sister is named. He was a great storyteller, they say, the sort of man that was rare – kind, and full of wisdom.

I remember my grandmother well. My earliest memory is from her house in Jerusalem, to which we had come, from Canada, for the unveiling of my grandfather's tombstone. I remember my baby sister there, crying in the middle of the night, and my exhausted mother comforting her. I often walk by that house for nostalgia's sake . . .

My father was raised in Winnipeg, Canada, on Zionistic idealism. My mother, at the age of seventeen, was required to spend a year in Israel to prove that she was Zionistic enough to marry my father, who planned to come and live here. During that time the 1956 Sinai War broke out, but she remained. There are home-movies of my aunt, my cousins, my father in a leather jacket, all holding shovels, working on a northern kibbutz. The secular builders of the holy land . . .

Somewhere the dreams, and the dreamers, vanished . . . My upstairs aunt and her family moved to the US in search of a job . . . My grandmother died. My father (re-)married an Israeli, and brought her and half her family to Canada, and he now criticizes Israel, its government, its problems, from a comfortable home far away. My other aunt and her husband, living on a farm near Haifa . . . are trying to buy a store on Vancouver Island. They do not light Shabbat candles. They safeguard their Canadian passports. And their beings reek of disillusion. Israel is a woman scorned by all her lovers . . .

Yet somehow I stumbled into this place . . . which I love as much as I love any person I know, which is the only place I can live . . . I alone remain of their dream. I alone have claimed my inheritance.

A few weeks later her father's reply reached Jerusalem.

My dearest [daughter],

I received your piece on historical reminiscences, and liked it, of course. I didn't find it harsh or an indictment because it doesn't consider the facts and circumstances which led to the lapsed dreams. It is, as it should be, a wonderful view from your present perspective – full of love and feeling and significant memory . . . It seems to me that your love of the country is anchored in history and in your religious view. Everything fits and I can understand and to a degree empathize with your feelings. However, the dreams of my sisters and mine were grounded in quite different things. My father was like you, wise and steeped in history and Torah, and this led to his wanting to be there. He would be appalled at what is going on internally now – and I am not so sure he would be as accepting as you are . . . This [Canada] is a money-grabbing, materialistic and alienated society (and was then as well). Israel of the '50s offered an alternative. The chalutzim [pioneer Zionists] had a vision, and that led to an energy and an impetus and a sense of national co-operation that was wonderful to experience. There was a sense of equality, excitement and a common goal. It was hard economically, but that was true across the board and because there was a vision, it was tolerable. What have we now – a materialistic, money-grabbing society, even worse than here – internal dissensions and hatreds, a huge disparity in economic well-being and, worst of all, *no* national vision and goal. So for us, what is the point? Can you understand why your aunt's family 'reeks of disillusionment'?

For twenty five years she has had to scrape, save, slave and suffer. For what? If you have just yourself to consider, you can make your way – especially someone like you, with your qualities, priorities and personal convictions. But how about those with family responsibilities, lack of wherewithal – losing sons, anxieties of war? Up until the early '80s, this could all be justified; but Lebanon and Sharon changed all that. What I am trying to say is that your piece doesn't account for the *why* of the disillusionment.

. . . You comment about my criticizing Israel from my comfortable home far away. That is true, I do. It is mainly from a sense of frustration and what I view as opportunities lost. And anyway, what is wrong with criticism? If it is constructive it can be positive. And at the very least, it shows that I still care.

Now let me share with you some of my feelings about the country. As you know I have visited many times, and have experienced with deep sadness what I regard as the degradation of the country. No, not the country, which I still love, but the people in it. How can I justify to myself, not to mention to my friends, the rabid right-wingedness of West Bank settlers? How can I justify, again to myself, Israel's Vietnam in Lebanon? I find it difficult to be comfortable with Israelis – many of whom have large chips on their shoulders and who are constantly disparaging anything outside themselves. Why do you think I shun the large group of Israeli visitors who come to Vancouver to accumulate a nest egg, who spend much of their time shitting on the city, its institutions and its way of life? How about that aspect of criticism and judgementalism?

And in spite of all this, I seriously plan to retire there . . . In spite of everything I've written, you have no idea how thrilled I am by your decision to settle in Jerusalem . . .

I love you very much. Dad.

Since the creation of the state of Israel in 1948 the fluctuations in the numbers of Jewish immigrants have been considerable. In 1949, for example, the total was 240,000; four years later it was just 10,000. Nothing has happened in recent years anywhere in the Middle East to compare with the size of the mass migration of Soviet Jews to Israel which began at the end of 1989; it was the combined result of the Soviet authorities relaxing emigration restrictions, and the United States (the preferred destination for most Jewish *émigrés*) cutting down sharply on the numbers being granted entry permits. Estimates of the total number of Soviet Jews who will arrive eventually in Israel varied in those early months of mass immigration. But as an indicator of the numbers involved, 10,500 arrived in April 1990, making it obvious that the total would be in the realms of many hundreds of thousands. Sufficient for President Chaim Herzog, in his address to the nation in that same month marking Independence Day, to speak of Israel having been 'graced by the occurrence of a miracle'.

This sudden mass migration of Jews, combined with the collapse of the communist regimes of Eastern Europe (which traditionally supported the Arab states in the Middle East conflict), left the Arab world in a state of shock and alarm. It was expressed in fears that the new immigrants would be settled in the Occupied Territories, thereby making Israel's hold on them irreversible. But the underlying worry was that the boost to the size of the Jewish population of Israel would be matched with a boost to the self-confidence of the nation as a whole at a time of sagging morale. That in turn, the Arabs feared, would be translated into a greater Israeli resolve to stand firm in the face of international pressure to work for a compromise settlement of the Middle East conflict.

That was certainly how 'the miracle' was viewed by a large section of Israelis. But amid the euphoria one could also hear voices of caution, indeed voices of warning. President Herzog spoke of 'shortcomings in our ranks – unnecessary difficulties, defects, neglect . . . One thing is certain: Jewish history will never forgive us if we fail to live up to the greatness of this hour.'

Housing and jobs: both had to be found urgently for the new arrivals, and neither (particularly the latter) was in abundance, since the economy was in poor shape. Hinda Geiman, a Soviet Jew who arrived in Israel fifteen years ago, told me that she and the rest of the Russian community were 'very, very worried at the prospects. For the people who come from Russia, work is central. The honour of being able to work and have a good job and being able to support yourself and not have to live on hand-outs from other people is more important than having an apartment to live in. You can get by, as you did there, with a family of four people in two small rooms. We lived that way [in the Soviet Union] and we were happy. The only thing is that we felt bad as Jews, and the government was ugly.'

Shmuel Lahis, of the organization trying to stem migration from Israel, also does not relish the idea of young Israelis being forced to compete for jobs when they come out of the army with new Soviet immigrants, many of whom are highly skilled. The outcome, he fears, is that 'many Israelis will leave'. A similar note of warning was sounded by Daniel J. Elazar of the Jerusalem Center for Public Affairs, writing in the *Jerusalem Post*. While welcoming the mass immigration as 'a boon . . . for the fulfilment of the Zionist dream and in our battle for survival,' he added the following words of caution:

> At the same time as we very properly rush to do our utmost to welcome and resettle our Soviet Jewish brethren, we must make every effort not to do so at the expense of our own native-born younger generation – those young people who were raised in this country, attended its schools, have become part of the very fabric of its culture and society, have given their years of service in the Israel Defence Forces and, in the process, postponed their own personal careers and lives to serve the national interest.

If these youngsters feel that their country is not offering them sufficient opportunities, Daniel J. Elazar concludes, 'they will do what all too many are already doing, namely, look for greener pastures elsewhere.'

Another point is that a sizeable proportion (how big, it's impossible to say) of new Soviet immigrants did not want to come to Israel in the first place. Their attachment to the ideals of Zionism or even to Judaism is weak, and if they find that jobs are not available they will hope for the chance to move on. That was certainly the view of a number of new arrivals interviewed in the early phase of the mass immigration. In other words, if there is not a giant capital investment from abroad to create new jobs, then Israel will have a major problem on its hands; and it is a problem that in some ways mirrors (not in its cause but in its effect) the difficulties faced by countries like Jordan and Egypt because of the economic recession in the Gulf states. And in the Middle East the unemployed, and others in society who feel frustrated, are often easy targets for religious fundamentalism. It's no coincidence that ultra-orthodox Jewish groups have begun trying to provide 'spiritual' support for the newly expanded Russian community.

Economic difficulties of one kind or another are shared by most countries in the Middle East; and the new immigrant to Israel will soon discover those that afflict the Jewish state. He will hear, for example, about the shortage of jobs for teachers, but at the same time he will learn that school hours are being cut because there's not enough money to keep a particular school open; and that, as we have seen, those parents who can afford it are contributing out of their own pockets to pay teachers to give extra classes – the 'grey education' syndrome. I learned of one mathematics teacher – married with four children – who, on top of his first job, gave private lessons in the afternoon and evening, and also got up at four in the morning to deliver papers before school. As I mentioned in the opening chapter, for many Israelis life is hard.

But this view is challenged by some of the old-timers, the early pioneer immigrants. Norman Cohen (who was in Palestine before the creation of the state) believes that 'many of the recent immigrants look at things in terms of what they had and therefore what they expect. They think we should take their advice, their expertise and so on. In the '40s, many of us who came then, came not with a feeling that we were going to save the country, but that we were going to live here.' Shulamit Berger (arrived 1949) also disagrees with the view that life today is hard. 'Not now, it's not. I think new immigrants who have waited so long to come have higher expectations; and I suppose because some people have it good, then others find it harder to overcome the hardships.'

Gidon Grader is a lecturer at the Israel Institute of Technology in Haifa, the Technion. He's in his thirties, and he and his young family had been in the country only a few months when I met him. He had the perspective of someone who had been born in Israel but had spent most of his life from his teens onwards in the United States. However, he came back to Israel for three years to serve in the army (where he met his wife), and never wavered in his certainty that one day he would live in Israel, and would stay. But he admits that the economy in Israel is in serious difficulties. He ascribes the problem to the fact that 'it's an old system built for a truly socialistic country which is a very nice ideal. But it's a system that doesn't compete well in today's world. And in today's world you simply can't be an island, you have to participate and compete with other countries and sell goods abroad. Especially a country like Israel which doesn't have many resources, so it has to import, process and sell; and if it can't do it efficiently, it won't be able to survive. As long as you have this cushion that America is supplying [millions of dollars' worth of aid each year] you're OK. But you're a dreamer if you think it will last into the future.'

Gidon Grader is in Israel because he is a hundred per cent a dedicated Zionist. He knows well the country to which he has committed himself. This is not the case with everyone coming to Israel. Many, like the Jews from Ethiopia, had a religious vision of the country in naive terms; but little more. Israel was a refuge in an unknown world. For others, Israel is the desired destination, even though they may know little or nothing about it when they arrive. This is the case with many of the Soviet immigrants, recent and not so recent. For every new arrival the prospect ahead is of 'becoming an Israeli'. And this happens to a greater or lesser extent, depending on the personality and background of the individual.

Hinda Geiman's big brown eyes filled with tears the instant I asked her to describe the day, fifteen years earlier, on which she and her family had left their home in Riga, in Latvia, to emigrate to Israel. 'Even now it makes me emotional, because I loved my city; but I felt like a stranger inside it. I really, really loved it, and still do. And I'm afraid to go back there because I don't want to bring back all the feelings, all the emotions of all the good times that I had in my youth. And anyway it was a jump to a strange country and a culture we didn't know. Without the language.' Before getting here the Geiman family say they had almost no idea of what Israel would be like, although a friend who had preceded them had written, giving them some information. The letter from the friend contained the following enigmatic advice: 'Be prepared for the fact that Israel is also part of the "East".' Hinda Geiman smiled as she told me this.

When the Geiman family arrived their absorption went smoothly, mainly because Hinda, who is a mathematician, was offered without delay a job in the Hebrew University by another Soviet émigré, a distinguished professor. And so she received the support which new immigrants from the Soviet Union need in showing them how a capitalist society works. They were also lucky in finding distant members of their family, Zionists from the early days, who received them warmly. 'They never said to us what other people said which was: "You've just come? Well, go to the desert to work." But there were a lot of other people who said things like that. Even the professor I knew, who was a professor of international stature, was told: "You came now? Go and teach in the Negev desert, we need to develop schools in the Negev." Despite the fact that he was making such great contributions to the university. And that's not an isolated incident.'

Several recent immigrants, or would-be immigrants, to Israel have told me of coolness and even hostility directed at them as newcomers. Resentment is based on the fact that they have not been paying taxes there, and have arrived after the hard work of settling the land and building up the infrastructure has been done, and when the wars have been fought. This feeling seems to be directed above all at Jews from northern Europe and the United States, where life is assumed to be easy; some Israelis feel that Jews from these areas are patronizing, and conduct a condescending flirtation with the Jewish state without giving total commitment to it.

The Geimans, like many other Russian Jews, had had no experience of any life outside the Soviet Union. Adapting to the social and cultural ways of a new country for the very first time is bound to be difficult, especially in a country like Israel with its diverse mix of people and cultures. Ginda Heiman said she was pleasantly surprised to find people open in their attitudes and 'always willing to help'. Here she paused and added, laughing: 'In principle.' But did she find it, as her friend had predicted, part of the 'East'? 'Oh yes,' she replied quickly, 'it's really the East.' What about the attitude of fatalism which newcomers often notice? 'Yes, it's part of the Easternness. We found, unfortunately, that a very large proportion of the population – they don't care, they're apathetic. What will be, will be. But we don't think that way, and we didn't absorb that way of thinking and we won't absorb that way of thinking.'

The Geimans' home is a flat in an austere modern complex in Gilo, a sprawling and soulless satellite suburb of Jerusalem built on land occupied by Israel in the 1967 Middle East War. The neighbourhood commands wonderful views of the city. Their flat contains many reminders of Latvia: paintings and photographs on the walls, dozens of Russian books on the shelves, and finely painted miniature Russian dolls and a miniature samovar in a display cabinet. The parents insist that Russian is spoken within the family, but their eldest son, having spent six years in the army, is now settled in a job in Jerusalem, and their second son, a teenager, has blended into his school surroundings. Their mother admits that 'both of them are Israeli, and society accepts them as Israelis. The younger one doesn't even look like a Russian, he's dark like a Moroccan.' And she laughs. She clearly realizes that, despite the cultural and linguistic ties with Europe, her sons are becoming part of the Middle

East.

One of the pictures on the wall in the Geiman flat is by Alexander Okun, who is another, more recent, *émigré* from the Soviet Union. His studio is in a bare rented room in a stark and ugly modern warehouse complex on the western fringes of Jerusalem. Alexander Okun left Leningrad because of the lack of freedom there, but still loves the city of his birth. We sat among a jumble of canvases, paints, trestles and easels in the chaos of the darkened studio to talk about the process by which Soviet Jews become Israelis. For Alexander Okun, the most important experience – aside from not having to be conscious of the Jewishness which set him apart from most other people in Leningrad – has been the excitement of taking part in the cultural development of a new country. Some of his works reflect a fusion of the style of the traditional Russian icon with an exploration of the themes of Jewish history and Jewish culture. Israel, he says, is still only in its forties; and that is not yet old enough for an indigenous culture to have emerged. He speaks of himself as a product 'of Soviet, not Jewish, culture'. Other artists are bringing influences from elsewhere into 'this great boiling pot. In 300 years we will see what kind of art emerges. Today everyone has the fantastic possibility to be a founding father.'

Alexander Okun's enthusiasm for Israel is shared by another even more recent immigrant, Neville Alexander, who arrived from London in 1986. He still has not been fully absorbed into Israeli society; he speaks only a little Hebrew, and relies for news on English-language broadcasts and publications. But he runs a pottery business in one of the new suburbs of Jerusalem, and believes it is important for new immigrants to have a positive view of their role in society. 'Everyone is needed because the country needs people. Particularly people who don't expect to be given a job and endless resources, and who don't wait for things to be put on their laps. We want to demonstrate that not all olim [immigrants] are arriving penniless and saying, "I want help, give me a job, I want security." If we'd come to Israel earlier we might have gone in to drain the swamps; but the swamps have been drained. We're creating employment.'

Others Jews come to Israel and delay as long as possible the decision about whether or not they're going to stay to become citizens of the Jewish state. Others, too, become Israelis, but keep their involvement and commitment at a distance. Jeremy Berkowits is an accountant who came to Israel eight years ago on holiday; he liked the country, so stayed on. He's religious, and in Britain was a full-time cantor in a synagogue. He says it's a convenient lifestyle for him in many respects – it's easier in Israel, for example, to keep a kosher house than it is in England. But if a good work offer came from the United States, he and his family would happily set up home there. 'We go back to the United Kingdom once, usually twice, a year and stay for three or four weeks. I still support Manchester United, and I'm in touch with house prices, sterling, the budget. I still feel absolutely British . . . We have very few Israeli friends, so I hardly speak Hebrew. My financial Hebrew and investment Hebrew is superb, but when it comes to dinner parties I don't know so much. We speak only English at home . . . One of the tests of commitment is whether you avoid serving in the army. I did serve, but only for two months because that was the minimum they requested. I feel a basic level of commitment, so I wouldn't shirk any duty requested of me; but I wouldn't go chasing any new ones.'

Serving in the army is necessarily part of the process of trying to understand the complexity of the Arab–Israeli dispute – the problem of the Palestinians and the Occupied Territories – which every new immigrant has to undergo. Jeremy Berkowits is physically closer to the dispute than many of his compatriots because, as an accountant, he is in the unusual position of being the only Israeli employee in an hotel in East Jerusalem which is staffed mainly by Palestinians. He says this hasn't presented difficulties, despite the assumption of some of his friends that it would. On only one occasion has he stayed away from work: that was when a Palestinian friend of his in the maintenance department at the hotel was beaten up by the para-military border police. 'My friend admits he provoked the border policeman who then knocked the hell out of him. What they did to him was foul. The next day I felt I couldn't come. Not because I was scared, but because I couldn't look him in the face.'

Immigrants will soon learn, too, that the Israeli attitude to the conflict with the Arabs, and particularly to the Intifada, is bound up with Israel's image in the world. Jeremy Berkowits's views on the subject put him into the category, judging from my own experience, of a very small minority. 'I think Israel gets a fair press. It gets the press it deserves. I think if they go around beating people up they should expect the press to report on it. It's ridiculous to say, for example, that Amnesty International or the BBC is biased against us. As long as the actual incidents are reported fairly. But nobody agrees with me.'

133

If not 'nobody', then certainly very few. The overwhelming majority of
Israelis would agree with Gidon Grader at the Technion in Haifa who
believes that Israel's image 'in the Western world is clearly changing, and
not to our favour. I think in large part it is the fault of the media. People
see numerous programmes in which we're not portrayed fairly, not even
portrayed equally to our neighbours. It's a serious problem. Part of it is
that reporters covering Syria or Lebanon don't find it so simple to collect
information. In Israel the media is very free to inform the world and show
all the problems. People say: "Syria must be quite a peaceful place, we
don't hear anything about it." I only wish that every time they showed the
troubles in the West Bank – and there's certainly not a desirable situation
there – they'd also show a clip from a Syrian town that's been wiped out
by tanks because the people there happen to disagree with the leaders of
the country.'

In my experience, too, most Israelis would also probably agree with
Gidon Grader's reply to my question about whether or not he thought the
Arabs as a whole still wanted to push Israel into the sea. 'Perhaps they
think it's going to be a little harder than they expected twenty years ago.
But they're certainly working on it.' A firm 'Yes' was the immediate reply
of Hinda Geiman to this same question. 'That was always their point of
view, it hasn't changed.'

Hinda Geiman says that her experience leads her to conclude that
almost all the Russian immigrants who come to the country immediately
become right-wing in their views. Gradually, these views shift a little
towards the centre. Anton Nossik, a doctor in Moscow before coming to
Israel, now works as a translator. Speaking after two months in Israel he
too was in no doubt that the arrival of so many Soviet Jews would give an
enormous boost to the parties on the right. 'The socialism offered by
parties like Labour and so on is very well known to the people who've
come from Russia. We know its low efficiency, its incompatibility with
human nature; and we'll be determined to vote against it. Also we'll be
determined to vote against the communists – and if it were possible we'd
vote for banning them altogether. Communists from our viewpoint are
no better than fascists. Soviet immigrants can be found on the far right of
the political spectrum.' Anton Nossik believes that these immigrants will
enable a strong right-wing government to run Israel without being
constrained by the smaller parties, and he is equally sure that this
government most certainly will not talk to the PLO ('they know Yasser

Arafat from Moscow – he was welcome there') or surrender control of the Occupied Territories.

Natalie Gurski arrived from Odessa just before the big wave of Soviet immigration. Arab worries, she says, are understandable. 'If I were an Arab I also wouldn't be too ecstatic about our arrival here, I wouldn't think it was too good for me personally. Because we, the ones who're coming here to Israel, are very right-wing in our political sympathies. And there's a reason for this. We're different from many Israelis; we've lived through all the pogroms and the Holocaust and all the things the local Jewry don't have any notion of. . . . We know from Russia all the attributes of socialism and are definitely not voting for it. As for the Arabs, I think they could behave differently. I can't feel too much affection for people who throw stones at my bus when it's passing Hebron. The people who endanger my life and the life of my children don't arouse much sympathy within me.'

Some political observers in Israel do not accept the assumption that the arrival of the Soviet immigrants will result in a surge of support for parties on the right. Given the fact, they say, that many of the new arrivals had no strong religious or ideological commitment to the Jewish state before they arrived, the chances were that the votes will be spread across the political spectrum, and an opinion poll published by *Ha'aretz* newspaper midway through 1990 backed this view. However, in direct contact with new Russian immigrants. I found no evidence to support this assessment – and given the very large numbers of Soviet immigrants arriving in the country in the early years of the decade, and given the prevailing rightward-tilting trend within the Jewish state, the chances of a majority of Israelis in the near future supporting a platform calling for moderation and flexibility in relations with the Arabs seemed remote. Especially since the very arrival of these immigrants was being interpreted by the Arabs as a sign that Israel was building up both its defensive barriers and its capability of holding on to the Occupied Territories through force of numbers. Yet another opportunity, then, for rhetoric of the Middle East to drown the voices of reason.

Much will depend on the performance of Israeli politicians. It seems that it doesn't take immigrants long, even immigrants from the Soviet Union where the democratic tradition is only just being born, to spot the glaring flaws in the Israeli system and to recognize the self-centred behaviour of most of the politicians for what it is.

'I can't respect our politicians,' the artist Alexander Okun told me, 'and we have an awful, awful system.' Gidon Grader, for all his enthusiasm and optimism about the future of Israel, is puzzled by the behaviour of the politicians, and by their ability to survive despite the contempt in which they are held. 'The same people are painting the scenery year after year. There's very little change in the political scene. Rabin and Peres, for example, just seem to be lasting for ever, and it's hard to say whether you'll see a drastic change from people who've been in the system for so many years. The country is more polarized now than it used to be, it's facing very difficult economic and political problems. People are in such a difficult state, it's natural for extreme ideas to flourish . . . There are phenomena for which I just don't have an explanation. For instance, the Lebanon War, which clearly wasn't in our favour – we lost many people, we didn't achieve our goals, it wasn't a necessary war – yet after the war the party which led us into Lebanon and the people who were responsible for it were re-elected immediately. It's almost as though the political parties are like a football team. You keep supporting them even though they've lost a game.'

But however contemptible the politicians may seem in the eyes of the electorate, new Israelis soon find themselves following each twist and turn of political events. They soon become addicts of newspapers and news broadcasts, like everyone else in the country. They become used to the sounds of helicopters and the sounds of air force jets, to the aggressive driving and irritable queue-barging, and to the lumpen indifference at the supermarket check-out. In a word, they learn, as Orielle Berry described it just before leaving Israel to live in South Africa, 'how to live on their nerves. It's so terrible. You've mentioned it, but we just take it for granted. It's not until you're out of here that you realize every other country is different. Even in South Africa there are no army radio broadcasts.' A 'pressure-cooker' was how Norman Cohen described Israel. 'It's hard to bring up children in this atmosphere. It's ridiculous – I can't eat my lunch if I haven't seen the newspaper. If you want to relax you have to get out of the country.' His wife Chana agrees: 'It's unbelievable how often people go away. Fifteen, twenty years ago very few people were able to or wanted to go. Now, our neighbours, immigrants from Iraq who came here in the early '50s, they all pay on the never-never and travel, all the time. We try to get away once in two years.'

Ehud Offer, an artist in his thirties, was born in Israel, studied art in

Boston, lives in the picturesque village of Ein Kerem tucked into the hills on the edge of Jerusalem, and has no intention of emigrating. 'I am an Israeli animal so I can't live in another country. I don't like people leaving when things get tough. If everyone leaves, then what happens?' He says he doesn't even go abroad on trips. 'But Israelis do feel the need to get out to forget everything, not to listen to the news, to clean the mind . . . Because life here is so tough sometimes I try to fly far away from it and fantasize through my pictures. All the time everything is in a political mess. You are embarrassed and confused. Unless you make a revolution here you can't change the situation. I'm not naive – I can't make the revolution, so I try to reflect the life here in my paintings. My art is very strong and very aggressive.'

Strength and aggressiveness are qualities which all the countries involved in the Middle East conflict will have to go on developing as long as that conflict remains unresolved. And it will fall to the citizens of the region to find ways of releasing some of the steam from the pressure-cooker from time to time if they are to survive. For many Israelis there is always the possibility of visiting friends and relatives in their countries of origin, even if those countries are situated behind what was once called the Iron Curtain. But for much of the Sephardi population – for the Jews from Iraq, Iran, Syria, Yemen and other countries in the Middle East – that option does not exist. For the Sephardis, Israel may be the Promised Land, but first and foremost it is home, and the only home they have. They are determined, furthermore, to have a say in how that home is organized and governed.

CHAPTER EIGHT

Jews of the Middle East

'A different mentality, but no great problem' – that was the neat summary one Israeli lady gave me when I asked her about the relationship between the Ashkenazi and Sephardi communities in the Jewish state. She was in a good position to judge: her father and mother were both immigrants, one from Yemen, the other from Romania.

I wondered more than once during my time in Israel – hearing, for example, that a quarter of all marriages these days bring together individuals from the two communities – whether the outside world was correct in assuming that such a division still existed. 'Israel is a melting-pot': if I heard it once, I heard it a hundred times. It is my belief that the young Israelis who are poured out of that pot are increasingly acquiring the characteristics and attitudes of the Middle East, in large measure because of the influence of the Sephardi community. The Sephardis' stamp on daily life in Israel is unmistakable.

The pulse of the Middle East is never far away – even at five-thirty in the morning, when, despite the early hour, the taxi driver sounded his horn sharply to announce his presence, and we headed out of Jerusalem towards the airport at Tel Aviv, under a colourless, invisible, dawn sky. As we came out of the wooded hills on to the slope leading down to the coastal plain, the sky over my right shoulder was filling with colour, revealing wisps of cloud; and with the inside of the car hazy with cigarette smoke and the taut quarter-tones of a Middle Eastern Israeli song, I was caught for a moment in a shaft of memory. I was once again, as happened on many occasions, in a taxi on the road out of Amman at dawn, with the signs of the sun about to appear on the horizon and with cigarette smoke and quarter-tones filling my head, on the way to catch the early flight to Beirut. So I wondered yet again, as I experienced another criss-crossing pattern of Middle Eastern sensations, whether labels like 'Sephardi' and 'Ashkenazi' were becoming obsolete? 'It's high time to stop dividing our nation according to origins,' a correspondent had complained in a letter to the *Jerusalem Post*. Perhaps he was right.

But the truth is that the distinctions have not been eradicated – not yet, at least. Otherwise there would be no need for the calls which are still made, for example, for more 'Oriental' music to be heard on the radio and for more Sephardi faces to be seen on television. The distinctions are still there, even if there is 'no great problem' and there is some confusion over the definition of exactly who is a Sephardi.

The label Sephardi is one of convenience, of short-hand. The true Sephardis are the descendants of the Jews expelled from Spain in 1492, 'Sephared' being the name for Spain in Hebrew. Many of them settled in areas which are now Bulgaria, Turkey and Greece; but they have kept alive their language, Ladino, which is a dialect of Spanish with Hebrew mixed in. Some Jews from Spain also moved to North Africa and other areas of the Middle East. These days all the 'true' Sephardis are lumped together with Jews from Muslim countries (including those whose families were living in the eastern Mediterranean centuries before the creation of Israel). They are all called Sephardi or, equally commonly, Oriental Jews, even though that term covers Jews from the Atlantic coast in the west through to the Indian sub-continent in the east. The confusion arises with the Jews from Bulgaria and Greece, who, strictly speaking, are Sephardis, their families having come originally from Spain, but who are almost always considered in the same bracket as Jews from Europe because of their centuries of contact with the West.

The problems between the Ashkenazi and Oriental communities in the days shortly after the creation of the state stemmed, as mentioned in the first chapter, from the latter's arrival in a society both created and dominated by the former. The Ashkenazis, mainly from countries like Poland, Russia and Germany, had had no contact with Oriental Jewry, and showed little inclination to learn about their traditions or to incorporate them into the new state. One old-timer from the United States recalled seeing a group of immigrants from Yemen being brought from Aden in the early days of the state. 'The first thing was to spray them with disinfectant for trachoma. They were beautiful people with gorgeous coloured clothes. And the clothes were taken from them. They weren't simply de-loused, they were taken. "Don't you want to look like Israelis?" we said. "Look at us in our khaki shorts." Not only did we lose treasures of national costume but we diminished them as a people.'

The Jews from Yemen or Morocco came from traditional male-dominated societies, and one can imagine that the transition into a society run by secular European Zionists was difficult. They felt excluded and humiliated. Large numbers were sent to remote agricultural settlements and new development towns. The economy was weak and jobs were few. 'Sometimes the wives were able to find work washing floors, or something,' the same old-timer told me. 'But often the father couldn't find a job. The children picked up Hebrew easily, but the father didn't. So the traditional authoritarian figure in the family was destroyed.'

When I spoke to members of the Sephardi community about those early days I found their memories were still dominated by the hardships. Levi Iyop came with his family to Israel from Iran in 1950. They emigrated, he said, because they wanted 'to return to our land, the land of Abraham, Isaac and Jacob.' But for the first sixteen years Levi had no proper job. Now he is elderly, slight in build and with grey hair and moustache and dark eyebrows. He owns a stall in the Mahane Yehuda market in Jerusalem; his grown-up son was doing the heavy work, carrying boxes of fruit out from the store-room, as the old man recalled the days when the family arrived from Iran, when they lived in tents and survived on bread.

Amira Levy is the only woman to own a stall in the same market. Born in Iraq, she was a child when she and her family arrived in Israel. But there is still a hint of guttural Arabic in her Hebrew speech, and she articulates with her hands in the Middle Eastern manner. Again, her earliest recollections are of 'very difficult times. There was rain, there were floods. We lived in tents and had no shoes. My father was rich when he was in Iraq. Here he was poor because there was no work. He managed to get a part-time job as a labourer.'

Because many of the Middle Eastern immigrants were sent to towns or agricultural communities in rural areas they found themselves often living close to a kibbutz and being dependent on it for labouring and other manual work. It does not require much imagination to understand how, to a Jew from North Africa or Yemen with little money and few prospects, the predominantly Ashkenazi kibbutzniks seemed to be leading a privileged and cushioned life. Looking over the fence into the neighbouring kibbutz from the meagre and soulless comfort of a development town it was a case, literally, of the grass seeming to be greener on the other side. It is hard to overstate the impact of experiences of this kind, which caused a deep-rooted hatred for and resentment of the Labour Establishment running the country. There was another factor, too. The new arrivals were sometimes the subject of scorn or abuse, accused of being boorish and primitive in their behaviour and attitudes. In fact they were sometimes dismissed contemptuously as being 'Arabs', with all the derogatory connotations which that word can contain in the minds of certain Israelis. And, as a Jew from North Africa remarked to me, 'To be perceived as an Arab when the country was engaged in a war with the Arabs was not a comfortable position to be in.'

The general election of 1977, which saw the Labour hold on power broken for the first time, marked the initial stage of the emergence of the Oriental community from the shadows of inferiority. Menachem Begin, who shocked the Labour Zionist Establishment by leading his Likud bloc to victory, was the hero of the Sephardi community. And despite the trauma of the war in Lebanon which destroyed his spirit and drove him into self-imposed exile in a modern four-bedroomed apartment on the western edge of Jerusalem, Menachem Begin remains the Sephardis' hero. Quite simply, he was the man who allowed the Oriental Israelis to take revenge on the old Labour Establishment.

The 1977 election showed that the Sephardis had political muscle, and under Menachem Begin members of their community began to move into positions of greater influence. Moshe Levy, an immigrant from Iraq, became the first Sephardi army Chief of Staff, an appointment which would have been unthinkable in the 1950s. David Levy from Morocco became a senior cabinet minister. The tide had started to turn. But the process of adjustment and change is clearly going to be lengthy: Oriental Israelis have made much bigger gains in local politics than they have on the national scene. Michel Abitbol, born in Casablanca in Morocco, is a professor at the Hebrew University in Jerusalem and an expert on North African Jewry. He says there is still a lingering feeling of inferiority and resentment 'that the Labour governments gave a disproportionate amount of money and help to the kibbutzim compared with their communities, because of ideological reasons. The majority of the Orientals support Likud, but they still regard Likud as an opposition party – even though the government has been in the hands of Likud [apart from the two years when Labour held the premiership under a rotation agreement with Likud in a national coalition] since 1977. But for these Jews, Begin is still in the opposition, and Peres, and Rabin and Ben-Gurion are still in office.'

It is not simply a matter of waiting for time to heal the scars caused by those feelings of inferiority. There are still clear indications of division between the Ashkenazi and Sephardi communities in Israel. Victor Azarya, an immigrant from Turkey and Professor of Sociology at the Hebrew University, says that even with a quarter of all marriages bringing the two communities together, and despite the 'melting-pot' process, it is too soon to say that the distinctions have been eradicated. 'Twenty-five per cent of mixed marriages still leaves you seventy-five per cent which aren't. These divisions still are important in society. I don't know what will happen in two or three generations, but I think they are still, and will continue to be, important for at least another generation ... This feeling of being marginal, left out, is still there. It has not been broken, even though people do feel that since Likud came to power there was a change in terms of the Sephardi Jews gaining some influence, some self-respect. There is still a big difference in levels of education, levels of high-prestige positions in society. And even if they do obtain more powerful positions in the government or in the parliament, or through the government in some kind of ministry, they are still very, very under-represented in the universities, in art and music, in the courts and the judicial system – all these positions which are considered to be "high-status". Politicians don't enjoy very high prestige.' The fact is, too, that the Oriental community has not made many inroads in to the major financial and economic institutions in Israel. There is still, therefore, a gap between expectation and fulfilment.

The change which has occurred is in the perception and definition of the divisions. They are not expressed in racist or ethnic terms: there is no 'race' problem in Israel. But as is the case in many other societies, racist attitudes surface in the humour – and despite all the changes, Jews from North Africa continue to be the subject of cruel jokes. For example: David Levy (the minister from Morocco) gets into a taxi. The driver turns round and says: 'Say, have you heard the latest David Levy joke . . .?' 'Before you go any further,' Levy chips in, 'I am David Levy.' 'Don't worry,' the driver says, 'I'll speak slowly.' Or: 'There are only two

Moroccan jokes. The rest are true.'

Humour apart, the divisions in Israeli society are viewed in terms of the socio-economic rather than the ethnic background – Professor Michel Abitbol says they are 'social, economic, educational and cultural divisions. Not racist.' It happens that a large percentage of those in the lower bracket in terms of education, income and economic prospects are Jews from Middle Eastern and African countries, and among this group there is widespread contempt for what is regarded as the intellectual élitism and snobbery of the (by implication Ashkenazi) academic world. Abitbol adds: 'I'm sure that many Sephardis consider me an Ashkenazi because of my position.'

Beersheba in southern Israel, on the edge of the Negev Desert, is a town where much of the population can be placed at the lower end of the socio-economic scale. With its wide dusty streets, unfinished buildings and flat, featureless surroundings it has something of the dispiriting feel of a small provincial town in Egypt. Michal Sudack is an immigrant from Canada. She and her husband are medical students and have lived in Beersheba for seven years. I asked her about the atmosphere in the town. 'The common culture is that of the Sephardi Jews. There's a lot of poverty and unemployment. There are chemical industries and the hospital, which has quite a few employees. And there's industry in Dimona [twenty miles away]. But people are hard up – it's not a recent thing, but it's not getting any better. There are quite a few drugs and some small crime. It's not a development town as such, but the atmosphere here is not a good atmosphere. It's sort of – it's the type of people and the lack of jobs and the amount of poverty. And there's a contrast between the university and the hospital people, and the rest of the people. Also it's very dirty and very ugly. It's a cycle of the people and the municipality. The latter build ugly houses, so the people don't like them. Nobody cleans up, so the city doesn't clean up. The city doesn't clean up so the people don't . . . This is not a very good neighbourhood. If the door [of the garbage bin cupboard] is shut, they won't open the door, they'll put the garbage on to the floor next to it. Maybe it's trivial things, but I think it says a lot about the people, about how they care about where they live. Their homes may be beautiful inside, but they don't care about the area around. I don't know if you can say it's a Sephardi attitude. I don't know how they lived where they lived. It's certainly low socio-economic.'

In other countries in the Middle East, such conditions and the mental attitudes associated with them have led to a revival of interest in religion. It should be no surprise, then, to hear of the same pattern emerging in Israel. One of the big shocks in the general election of November 1988 was the success of the ultra-orthodox party Shas in attracting votes from the Sephardi community, especially in the development towns where, in the view of Michel Abitbol 'the economic and social situations have worsened since the '70s'. Even a brief visit to such a town, like Bet She'an at the northern end of the Jordan valley or Dimona in the south, is sufficient to see that conditions are basic. These towns have an air of temporary aberrations on the landscape: rows of cheaply constructed apartment blocks, with wooden shutters hanging limply in a state of disrepair and with plaster peeling and chipped, and small scruffy clusters of shops. The groups of men hanging around the towns are proof of the employment difficulties. In Bet She'an one weekday morning I came upon a minor road accident in which two cars had collided. Given the time of day, a remarkable number of men and women of working age emerged from the surrounding buildings to make up the crowd of onlookers.

When the majority of Oriental Jews came to Israel in the early days of the state they remained too bewildered for years to understand the political, social, economic and religious patterns which they encountered. They were unable to put down roots in the Labour Zionist Establishment (which was secular and European in character), in the religious Zionist movement of the National Religious Party (which was also European-dominated), or in the ultra-orthodox group Agudat Israel. None of these groups offered a comfortable home for the Middle Eastern tradition of Judaism which differed considerably from that practised in Europe. Oriental Judaism is a more simple and relaxed expression of the religion, and has picked up some of the patriarchal traditions and colourful rituals particular to local areas of the Middle East and North Africa. I once asked a stall-holder in the market in Jerusalem whose family were immigrants from Iran about the significance of the hand made out of brass – the hamsa – which hung from the entrance to his shop and so many others round about. 'Oh, it's for luck,' he said, 'and to ward away the evil eye. As Jews we can't believe in the evil eye. But we guard against it – just in case.'

There is great reverence among Oriental Jewry for rabbis and other holy men (and their tombs), and a great emphasis on mysticism and folk-lore. In recent years large numbers of Jews of Middle Eastern origin (who, as we've seen, are so often at the bottom end of the socio-economic scale in Israel) have been rediscovering their religious roots. And these are not the religious roots of mainstream European Judaism on which Zionism was built; they are roots firmly embedded in the Middle East.

One particular Jewish festival and one particular centre of Jewish pilgrimage have been adopted by the Sephardi community as an occasion for a powerful and colourful display of self-expression, both religious and secular. The site is Meron in Galilee just west of Safed; the festival is Lag Ba'Omer which is a one-day break in the forty-nine-day mourning period between Passover and Pentecost. Meron is a pilgrimage site because it is where the tomb of Rabbi Shimon Bar Yochai is reputedly situated. The Rabbi hid from the Romans for thirteen years after the Bar Kochba revolt in the second century AD, during which time, according to folk tradition, he wrote the Zohar – the Book of Splendour – which is the basic text of Jewish cabbalistic mysticism. At the celebration of Lag Ba'Omer the tradition is to light bonfires, and on the evening of the festival fires can be seen all over Israel. But the celebrations in Meron have a character of their own.

In Meron you find yourself caught up in an atmosphere which is intoxicating, an atmosphere which is marked as much by religious fervour as it is by pagan abandon. Going to Meron at Lag Ba'Omer is like going into the *suq* in Cairo or Rabat. It takes you by the throat. Hundreds of thousands of people converge on a tomb on a wooded hillside in Galilee for a spiritual carnival. Your senses are assaulted on all sides as you progress slowly up the winding and dusty track towards the tomb. Pilgrims like to spend the night at Meron, and the first thing you notice as you approach are the patches of blue, orange and green of thousands of tents by the roadside, in the woods and dotted over the hill around the tomb. Then there are the bright colours of the ladies' clothes: shocking pink, red and orange catch the eye, as does the glint of gold. Among the men you see glimpses of dignified elegance – like the elderly man from Morocco, wearing a light-blue jalaba (the traditional full-length garment worn throughout North Africa) and a cream-coloured fez with a black tassel. And among the colours and fashions of the Middle East are the black coats and hats of the ultra-orthodox men. One coming away from the tomb was, incongruously, carrying a large suitcase. His wife, in smart clothes, looked uncomfortable picking her way forward in high heels in this dusty, and overpoweringly Middle Eastern setting.

This is a religious occasion, but also it's a bazaar. All the way up the track to the tomb there are stalls selling just about anything: holy candles, hair brushes, toy guns, screwdrivers, children's clothes (under a beach umbrella advertising Kent cigarettes), rugs with the face of the Rabbi of Lubavitch, the head of the world-wide Habad movement, woven into them, portraits of Rabbi Shimon Bar Yochai ('Only two shekels to have a righteous man in your house,' shouts an ultra-orthodox man holding up one of the pictures) – even ladies' underwear. 'How come you are selling ladies' underwear at the tomb of a holy man?' I enquired of the girl standing behind the upturned boxes which served as the display counter. 'Because people buy it,' was the curt reply. And in the thick of it, Oriental music blares from a dozen different sources, and loudspeaker voices urge people to come forward, give money and receive a blessing. These appeals are expressed in rhythmic chanting which is both wild and happy, and in the rhythmic rattling of collection boxes: 'Charity will save you from death,' was one call distinguishable in the cacophony.

I stood apart from the slowly moving crowd for a moment to try to take in more of what was happening. A large lady in a bright red, full-length dress, with a gold necklace, was sitting at a low trestle table sifting couscous, the traditional Moroccan staple food. Nearby a small boy from an ultra-orthodox family was sitting astride a low wall intently picking at the remnants of a grilled fish. A man walked by with a blue T-shirt and cut-off denims; his skin was dark and he wore a red fez with a gold star on the side. There was a girl with a T-shirt which read 'I love Buenos Aires'. A woman soldier, with reddish hair and pale skin, looked down at the scene below with blank astonishment. A youth in jeans walked by leading a sheep, on his way to an enclosure above the tomb where a crowd was watching sheep being slaughtered under the supervision of a black-coated rabbi, before being cleaned, skinned and prepared for cooking. The whole of the Meron area is covered by the haze of burning charcoal from tens of thousands of barbecues. The air is thick with the smell of smoke mixed sometimes with incense, at other times with the odour of putrid flesh. I had heard that animal sacrifices were performed at Meron – clearly some families had performed their own ritual slaughters and had left the remains of the animals to rot in the ditches.

Overall there was a sense of celebration. It was a time for eating, drinking and dancing. I watched one ultra-orthodox man perform a spontaneous dance with his hands raised while balancing a metal collection-box on his head. The crowd round about clapped and laughed. Ululations rose from a group of women as a young child with red hair was lifted up to have his first haircut – the locks were snipped off and popped into a plastic bag. There is a tradition in some Jewish communities of giving a male child his first haircut at the age of three at Meron. This is called the 'Hallaqa'.

On a rug under the trees I met Pinchas and Hannah Zacchariah, an elderly couple who came to Israel from Iraq in 1951 and live in Tiberias. They visit Meron every year. I asked Hannah what its significance was for her. She kissed the palm of her right hand and waved it in the direction of the tomb. 'It's a holy place. We believe very, very much that it will help us to come here on Lag Ba'Omer. It's good for luck, for prayers, for victory, for people who're sick, for everything. And you meet all kinds of people, and you see people. It's like a holiday, like a big birthday party.' At this point we were interrupted by the arrival of a 'holy man', a stooped ultra-orthodox figure with greying side-locks, wearing a striped silk coat. He and Hannah began talking, and she asked him for a blessing for her son serving in the Israeli army. The old man rocked back and forth over his stick mumbling his blessing. Hannah gave him money, and we continued our conversation.

'Ninety per cent of the people here are Sephardi,' Pinchas told me. 'The Sephardis like to go to all the different tombs. We went to the tomb of Rabbi Meir Ba'al Hanes ('The worker of miracles') in Tiberias and there were no Ashkenazis there. We like doing this sort of thing.' Meir Ochayon, a Moroccan immigrant living in Bet She'an, agreed. 'Most people here are Sephardis, because outside Israel we learnt about all the righteous men here like Rabbi Shimon Bar Yochai and Rabbi Meir Ba'al Hanes, and we all go to their tombs. It's very nice here, and you feel good.' Pinchas Zacchariah picked up this theme: 'The Iraqis and Moroccans are just looking for fun and good food. We don't want money because we have God. We work and we eat, that's it. Now please have something to drink with us . . .'

The resurgence of interest in religion has been mirrored in the countries which the Oriental community in Israel left behind, and elsewhere in the Middle East. The crushing defeat of the Arab states by Israel in 1967 led to the Pan-Arab socialism propagated by President Nasser of Egypt and others being wholly discredited. When the structure fell, the Arab people turned to religion for comfort. The reason for this trend among Oriental

Jews in Israel, in the view of Michel Abitbol, is 'the failure of universal ideologies like socialism, the Labour movement and so on. In certain ways, too, it's the failure of Zionism. . . . It's failed as an ideology. It created the state of Israel, but beyond this it failed to give an ideological course. Zionism was a very efficient operative before the creation of the state because its whole aim was that creation. And very few Zionist ideologists envisaged the situation after that. And for this failure, Israel returned to religion – not just Sephardi Jews, but all Israeli society.'

In Arab countries, Islamic fundamentalist groups have thrived in atmospheres of disillusion of this kind. In Egypt, for example, Islamic groups have stepped in to create a society within a society, to provide not just spiritual guidance but practical social help. Schools and clinics have been set up in towns and villages where the state has been unable to meet basic needs, for whatever reasons. When an Islamic group provides these services to a community in need, it's no wonder that many people within that community are attracted by the group's spiritual ideals. It is a similar story in Israel. One of the surprises of the general election of November 1988 was the success of the ultra-orthodox party, Shas, especially among the Sephardi community, much of which until then had shown little interest in religion and religious parties. It turned out that Shas had also been winning political votes by offering social and welfare assistance within the community. 'Shas was the first "ethnic" party', Michel Abitbol told me, 'which understood that in order to create very strong ties within society you have also to find means to reinforce the influence of the party on society. They were the first party to create schools [outside the normal system] for development towns, schools which take students from seven in the morning until six in the evening. In other words schools which would take care of children's needs all day [while their parents were at work] and which were therefore the main guarantee against drugs, crime, etc. And for these very important social functions Shas had made very big gains among the Sephardi Jewry, which didn't see it just as a political party, but as a party with a social dimension.'

While schools set up by Shas offer a religious-based education system, clubs organized by the party provide meeting-places and facilities for young people in deprived urban areas. The organizers of the clubs say their main aim is to provide 'a spiritual shelter', and this includes the teaching of Jewish traditions and Jewish values. The state schools, they argue, teach the facts about religion, but not its values. Secular Israelis are clearly concerned that the success of these clubs will mean more and more young people being attracted into the ultra-orthodox camp. But in the absence of state-provided facilities and in the light of a growing drug and crime problem they have little ammunition with which to counter the trend.

Shas won votes from the Oriental community at the expense, mainly, of Likud. But Likud still enjoys enormous support from the Sephardis. The majority of those I met at the religious pilgrimage at Meron said they were solidly behind Likud. When I asked for their views on Labour, one man made a sweeping dismissive gesture with his right hand and said: 'Labour is only good for the Arabs. Likud is good for the Jews.' Another said simply: 'They don't do anything for us. They don't like the Sephardis.'

As we have seen, David Levy is one of the big stars of the Oriental, and especially North African, community. He and others in Likud touch a nerve with the Oriental community, which prefers a mixture of down-to-earth homespun philosophy to logical thoughts of a European-style politician, the kind of politician who is still associated in the minds of the Sephardis with the Labour party. Labour has only recently and belatedly awoken to this fact. The Sephardis respond to strong leaders who declaim in the manner of demi-gods; they love the charisma and oratory of Ariel Sharon, just as they loved (and love) those of Menachem Begin. I remember, during a visit to Israel in 1984, attending a Likud rally just before polling day in the main square in Tel Aviv. The party leader, Yitzhak Shamir, looked small and insignificant behind the microphones on the podium. His audience heard him politely, but with little evident enthusiasm – except when he mentioned the name of Menachem Begin. Then the crowd roared and clapped its approval.

The Sephardi community are certainly not alone in Israel in wanting strong leadership. Their roots were formed in societies where democracy is the exception and authoritarianism, in whatever guise, is the rule. Unlike Israelis with roots in Europe, they have had scant contact with left-wing thinking. This fact, combined with the lingering resentment felt towards Labour, has tended to influence the Sephardis to vote for parties to the right of centre. But you seldom find the Oriental Israelis taking extreme positions, either on the far left or far right. Professor Victor Azarya explains: 'Both on the far left and the far right you find people who are much more educated, ideologically oriented and articulate in terms of their ideology than you will find in the centre. So both Tehiya on the one hand, and the Citizens' Rights Movement on the other, are groups which have Ashkenazi constituencies. On the other hand, if you look at the Kach movement [a group led by Rabbi Meir Kahane, a rabble-rousing American-born racist who advocates the expulsion of all Arabs] you find a large, very large, over-representation of Oriental Jews. Again, though, this is not because they are Oriental Jews as such – rather, it's because they come from the less-educated strata.'

This desire to be led, combined with the inherent Middle Eastern trait of fatalism, makes me certain that if strong leaders advocating peace and reconciliation with the neighbouring states were to emerge in the Middle East, the mass of the populations, as much in Syria and Iraq as in Israel, would be prepared to follow them. But with a drift towards the right in Israel and a growing clamour for religious fundamentalism in the whole region, such a prospect does not seem likely. And the longer the region has to wait for peace, the more entrenched each side in the conflict becomes.

In general the Sephardi community have a reputation for being hawkish in their attitude to the Arab-Israeli dispute, if not openly hostile to Arabs. A common view is that Jews who came from Middle Eastern countries have a deeply felt fear and distrust of Arabs because of their experiences in the region in the years before they came to Israel. Such a view is encouraged by those on the right in Israel who want to foster the image of Arabs as a bloodthirsty, untrustworthy and religiously intolerant people. But Professor Azarya disagrees with this thesis. Again, he says, it comes down to socio-economic backgrounds. 'The fact that most of the Oriental Jews are less educated puts them into the category of being "anti-Arab". We're mostly talking about the second generation of Sephardis, who were born here and don't have any experience of the Arab world. And I think that the experience of those who did live in Arab countries – except for a very short period in Iraq in 1948 and maybe in Libya for a few years – wasn't such a bad one. After all, Jews under Muslim rule always fared better than those under Christian rule. I really don't see that Jews under Muslim rule had the worse experience or that they see the Arabs as being more cruel and more dangerous than do the Jews who lived under Polish, German or Russian rule.'

Saul Bellow, in a book about Israel, *To Jerusalem and Back: a Personal Account*, talks of how 'these North African and Oriental Jews are blamed for bringing a baksheesh mentality to Israel'. Whether 'blame' is the right word is arguable, but beyond doubt the presence of the now-self-confident Sephardis and the blending of their spiritual and cultural background into the texture of Israeli society have accelerated the process by which the country has found itself increasingly welded to the Middle East. And this trend is bound to continue, given the generally high birth-rate among Oriental families. (A mainly Sephardi philanthropic organization called Hibbah – the movement for spreading Jewish heritage – has said that 'an exemplary' Israeli family is one which has between twelve and twenty children who serve, or will serve, in the army; they provide financial rewards for a chosen number of 'exemplary families' in this birth-rate category each year.)

The arrival of hundreds of thousands of immigrants from the Soviet Union will clearly boost the size of the Ashkenazi community, as well as increase the competition for jobs throughout the Israeli workforce. The Sephardis as a whole may be less squeezed than Israelis from the higher socio-economic strata, since the general level of education and training of the new Soviet immigrants is relatively high – though if the major cities (where most of the Russian Jews try to live) are the chief recipients of investment to create jobs, outlying agricultural settlements and development towns could find themselves even further out on a barren economic limb.

Locations like the central bus station in Tel Aviv or the Mahane Yehuda market in Jerusalem may already have the look and feel of the Middle East. But, as we have seen, there are still many areas of Israel where society is anything but Middle Eastern in character. I asked Victor Azarya, the Professor from Turkey, how much he felt Israel had become a state of the region. 'When I come back from the United States or from Europe I do feel that this is not a copy of those, it is a Middle Eastern country. But when I come back from Cairo or Istanbul I see that it has no resemblance to those cities either. However, much of the culture, language and way of living are affected by the Middle East.'

Israel as a whole may be in a process of adjustment and transition between West and East. But there are areas of the Jewish state which are islands of pure Middle Eastern society, both Muslim and Christian, even though the flag which flies over these communities, like any other in Israel, bears the Star of David, and despite the fact that these particular Muslims and Christians carry passports of the Jewish state.

CHAPTER NINE

Arabs of Israel – enemy within?

S HE came down from Haifa on the bus to see her cousin and some friends from her neighbourhood who were in their first year at university in Tel Aviv. They were all Israeli Arabs, and were happy to be together again. They went into a bar for a drink; they chatted excitedly and laughed a lot. The barman came over and spoke quietly to them in Hebrew. 'Please don't talk in Arabic,' he said. 'It upsets the customers.' Jewish Israelis, in my experience, acknowledge the existence of the three-quarters of a million Arabs within their population, but prefer to keep them at arm's length. In these days of Intifada violence in the Occupied Territories 'Arabs' can, more then ever before, mean potential violence. You aren't absolutely sure if the Arab from Haifa or Jaffa, whose quiescence and co-operation you took for granted in the past, is now involved in the emotions, and possibly the violence, of the Intifada. The Jewish community of Israel is right to be uncertain. The status of the Israeli Arab has become even more complicated, even more delicate.

One Israeli Arab told me: 'We are considered by the rest of the Arabs as Israelis. From the point of view of Israelis, though, we are Arabs.' He laughed. 'You see we lose both ways – it's a dilemma.'

Jews from Arab countries have integrated into Israeli society and are helping the process by which the complexion of Israel is becoming more Middle Eastern. The same cannot be said for Israeli Arabs. However, as we shall see, their presence has forced Israel to face up to Middle Eastern phenomena not just on its doorstep but deep within its own borders.

The Arabs of Israel carry Israeli passports and vote in Israeli elections, but they are a community apart. Since the founding of the state they have not been required to serve in the army because their loyalty to the Jewish state (even though there has been no reason thus far to doubt it) cannot be taken for granted, given that Israel's enemies are mostly within the Arab camp. They could not be expected to take up arms under the Israeli flag and shoot fellow Arabs, perhaps even relatives, serving in an Arab army. Most Israelis I spoke to had a blinkered view of their own Arab community. Was it discriminated against? 'Nonsense, They're better off here than they would be in any Arab country,' would be a summary of Jewish replies.

It is true that Palestinians living in the West Bank and Gaza Strip are treated more harshly than Arabs who live in Israel as loyal Israeli citizens, but precisely because those citizens are loyal, it seems to me, the contemptuous disregard with which they are treated at both official and unofficial levels brings discredit on the Jewish state. In their treatment of the Arab community the Israelis have fallen far short of the ideals contained in the Proclamation of Independence of 14 May 1948, which declared that the new state would be a democracy based 'on the foundations of freedom, justice and peace in the light of the vision of the Prophets; it will maintain complete social and political equality of rights for all its citizens regardless of religion, race and sex; it will guarantee freedom of religion, conscience, language, education and culture. . . .'

Not all Israelis refuse to confront the question of the Arab community. Some are unhappy and even embarrassed at their inferior status; others feel that a blinkered approach is dangerous. Dr Rafi Israeli, an expert on Israeli Arabs at the Hebrew University of Jerusalem says: 'I can see alarming signs that things are getting out of hand,' referring to a noticeable increase in support for Islamic fundamentalist groups within Arab communities in Israel. Was he saying, I wondered, that they were 'an enemy within,' an enemy inside the Jewish state? 'Yes, absolutely. There's no doubt about it.'

Palestinians in the Occupied Territories and elsewhere often feel that they are the one community within the Middle East which has been neglected by Arab and non-Arab alike. But they are centre-stage compared with the Palestinians of Israel. I am certain that many people within the Arab world, never mind the world outside, simply do not know that they exist. An Arab from Galilee told me how, travelling in Egypt, he mentioned to a Coptic Christian there that he lived in Israel. The Copt was taken aback, saying he'd never met a Jew before. He was not easily persuaded that the man opposite him was also a Christian, as well as an Israeli.

They are a forgotten people because they do not fit into any easily explicable category. When the hundreds of thousands of Palestinians left their land in 1948 (either because of direct force or because of fear), these families stayed behind. The fact that they later became Israeli citizens led Arabs outside to despise them for many years as collaborators with the Zionist authorities. For the Arabs of Israel themselves, it was the start of a long period of harsh adjustments, combined with political and cultural isolation from the rest of the Arab community. Large areas of agricultural land were confiscated by the authorities in the new Jewish state, and the Arab community as a whole had little choice but to accept the manual and service jobs offered them – a role that has changed little in the subsequent years. Until 1966 Arabs were forced to suffer the added humiliation of living under military administration (as their cousins in the West Bank and Gaza Strip have done since 1967) because they were considered a threat to security. In fact, events proved that they were not; and as long as they could be contained in their own communities (mostly in northern Israel) and sealed off from the heady air of Arab nationalism, the Israeli Arabs were considered manageable.

The Middle East War of June 1967 changed matters. The capture by Israel of East Jerusalem, along with the West Bank and Gaza, brought the Palestinians of Israel into direct contact once more with the Palestinians of the Territories. The Palestinian consciousness of Israeli Arabs began to be re-awakened. On 30 March 1976 six people were killed when Israeli security forces were sent in to break up a protest against the confiscation of Arab land in Galilee. For Israeli Arabs that day, subsequently known as Land Day, came to symbolize the injustice of the system to which they were expected to be loyal, and has been marked each year since by strikes and demonstrations – not just in Israel, but in Palestinian communities everywhere. I remember clearly the emotional scenes at the Arab university in Beirut in 1981 when Yasser Arafat addressed a huge Land Day rally. The emotive occasion called out the nationalistic and anti-Israeli invective of any other long-established anniversary. In other words, the events of Land Day 1976 had helped to link Palestinians living inside Israel with the Palestinian people as a whole, and more particularly with their nationalist struggle. No longer were the inhabitants of Galilee and elsewhere content to be refered to as 'Arabs' of Israel: now, once again, they felt they were full-blooded Palestinians. This rebirth of

Palestinian consciousness was accelerated by the Intifada, which began at the end of 1987, when questions of their identity and loyalty were suddenly brought into sharp focus.

'I am an Arab, a Palestinian, a Christian and a citizen of the state of Israel,' Canon Riah Abu el-Assal, the head of the Anglican Church in Nazareth told me. 'Little wonder that outsiders get confused. In the minds of most people "Arab" means "Muslim", and "Israeli" means "Jew". The fact that we are at the same time Palestinian and Israeli presents a crisis in our identity, and this is a real problem as far as loyalty is concerned.'

Khaula Abu Bakr is an educational counsellor and sociologist, whose family are Arab Israelis living in a Jewish Israeli neighbourhood in Acre. The result is a psychological strain: 'Sometimes I'm feeling that I'm falling apart. It's very difficult because I do understand what the Jews are going through and I do understand what the Palestinians in the West Bank and Gaza Strip are going through. I want to be a bridge between the two peoples. But a bridge is something people have to step on to get across and I feel we're being stepped on and hurt too much.'

The psychological strain has been particularly hard to bear in the period since the start of the Intifada because Arab Israelis have had to witness the suffering of their own people at the hands of the Israeli army in the Occupied Territories. Abdel Wahab Darawshe, one of the six Arab members of the Israeli Knesset, says the actions of the Israeli army have left an indelible impression on the Israeli Arab community. 'They did not expect that the army would behave in such a cruel way as they are doing in the Occupied Territories. And we are talking about our brothers there, they are part of us, part of our people. So when we see the army which belongs to our country, Israel, behaving in such a way through orders that they get from our government, we feel very angry about it, and it brings a lot of frustration and bitterness.'

At home in a town or village in Galilee, watching the television pictures of riots in the Occupied Territories and hearing the daily catalogue of deaths and injuries, quite apart from news of the social and economic upheaval there, has not been easy for the Palestinians of Israel. Khaula Abu Bakr lives in a block of flats overlooking the sea at Acre. As the sun set over the Mediterranean, a cooling breeze began to pick up, and the Intifada seemed part of another corner of the world. But in the mind of Khaula Abu Bakr it's a constant pinprick of guilt. 'I have family in two villages in the West Bank, one near Jenin, the other near Nablus. My cousins are there. A week ago one of my cousins got married, but I was afraid to go. My mother and my aunts wanted to go, but they too were afraid. In the end we decided to go for just one hour, and then we all came back with the bride and groom to celebrate here in Acre. The first thing I said when we got to their village was: "How can you live such a life?" It's like when I visited a friend in East Jerusalem and heard shooting. She said: "It's usual, the army are just letting people know they're there." When I got back home I felt: "What am I doing? How can I just sit here watching television and reading newspapers?"'

Khaula Abu Bakr once gave a lecture on how the Arabs of Israel were coping with the Intifada, and remembers being challenged by a Palestinian from the Gaza Strip. 'He thought I was defending Israel and saying that Palestinian Israelis should accept Israel as a state and not help Palestinians in the Territories. And I said the problem of Palestinians inside Israel was not the same as that of the Palestinians in the West Bank and Gaza Strip. Our problem is political, and we need to struggle for more rights and equal rights and political rights; and the problem in the Territories is one of occupation . . . But he thought I was a traitor, pro-Israeli and not pro-Palestinian. And I have the other problem with Jews – when I talk about the Palestinian problem they think I'm against Israel and pro-Palestinian. So we end up being traitors to both nations.'

Despite their loyalty to the Jewish state, the Arabs of Israel make no secret of their identification with the nationalistic aspirations of the inhabitants of the West Bank and Gaza Strip. They have mobilized political support for them, and have collected and distributed money, clothing and food. In towns and villages in Arab-dominated areas of Israel it is common to see Palestinian flags drawn on walls, accompanied by PLO slogans, and there have been some incidents of stone-throwing and other acts of nationalist-inspired violence. A schoolteacher told me that on Israel's Independence Day pupils at her school tore down the Israeli flag. Such acts of violence and defiance are rare, but when they have occurred they've been seized upon by right-wingers in Israel, who argue that the Intifada is spreading across the 1967 lines.

Scenes in Nazareth in May 1990 confirmed beliefs that the loyalty of the Israeli Arabs was in question and that tougher measures should be taken against them. What happened that month was that a lone Israeli gunman shot dead seven Palestinians from the Gaza Strip who were waiting early in the morning at Rishon Lezion near Tel Aviv, at a spot known popularly as the 'slave market', in the hope of getting work for the day. The killings caused an explosion of anger both in the Occupied Territories and within Arab communities in Israel. Israeli–Arab leaders called a strike. Protest marches were held, some of which ended in clashes with the police. The most serious disturbances were in Nazareth, where police used tear gas in a day of running skirmishes with groups of masked youths who threw stones, erected street barricades and set fire to buildings.

For an Israeli watching television news that evening, it was a shock: these were the kind of scenes he was accustomed to witnessing in film reports from Nablus or Hebron, not from a city within Israel itself. But to deduce from the events in this one town on this one particular day that the Intifada had spread to Israel would be incorrect. It was an expression of anger, mixed with nationalist and Islamic fundamentist emotions, but the trouble lacked the ferocity of similar scenes in the Occupied Territories. The police did not open fire; injuries were few – again there were signs of a balance between headstrong emotion and cold pragmatism. In the Occupied Territories such balance disappeared many years ago. In the Gaza Strip, on the same day as the protests against the Rishon Lezion murders, three Palestinians were shot dead by the army and more than a hundred were injured.

The overwhelming impression I have after talking to many Israeli Arabs is that while they support and identify with the aspirations of the Intifada, they have no intention of imitating what is happening in the West Bank and Gaza Strip. That is the view of Hanna Ibrahim, a tall and elegant Galilee poet. 'Yes, we are Palestinians but by this way, by throwing stones, we can't help those in the Territories. On the contrary we make things worse. Can we create a Palestinian state there by throwing stones here? We simply want to be treated as full citizens in Israel. We want equality with our brethren the Jews. We are discriminated against.'

Knesset member Abdel Wahab Darawshe agrees that to resort to violence would be counter-productive. 'I know that many extremist Jews are waiting for us to use violence, in order to justify their discrimination policies, and they will want to use it as an excuse to say: "Look, our Arabs after more than forty years are not loyal to Israel; so how can you believe a Palestinian state near Israel will live peacefully with us?" They will use it as an excuse to convince public opinion against establishing a Palestinian state near Israel. And we say: "We are Israeli citizens, we are loyal to our country; at the same time, we are Palestinians, loyal to our people. We want the real interests of both."'

There is no doubt that political groups on the far right in Israel, including those who favour the expulsion of the Arabs, would welcome an excuse to crack down on the community. Canon Riah says that Israelis have no grounds for accusing the Arabs of disloyalty, but the word 'loyalty' needs to be defined. 'If it's loyalty to the government that discriminates against us, then there's very little of that. If it's loyalty to the higher values of living and co-living, then I think the Palestinians here have done very well. And even if there should be a Palestinian state in the West Bank and Gaza Strip we'd continue to live in Israel and continue to struggle for equality as citizens of Israel.'

This attachment to the land, despite the fact that the land is now part of the Jewish state, is strong. The Arabs of Israel have overcome the humiliation of being branded traitors by their brethren outside for having stayed and co-operated with the Jewish state. Forty years and more later, while their cousins sit in refugee camps in Lebanon or Jordan, they at least are still on the land, they are the link with the land. Samir Nasser had a life in the United States, but decided to return to his village in Galilee to be close to his family roots. 'I want to stay here. My parents lived here, they were born here and died here. I'll stay here and die here. All the time that I talk with my kids we are Palestinians, our language is Arabic. This is our land.'

You step into a different world when you enter Arab areas of Israel. You leave behind the smart villas or densely packed junk-built blocks of flats which dominate the Jewish towns on the coast. As you rise up towards the hills of Galilee the buildings become more squat, with flat roofs. Mosques dominate the skylines of the towns and villages, which sprawl haphazardly and untidily outwards from the centre. Buildings of random size and design are littered over the landscape, some slotted into hillsides, supported by stilts. The land seems harsher, wilder, less cultivated than in Jewish areas. But the buildings, in all their lack of conformity, seem comfortable in the landscape, more comfortable than either the fortress-like blocks of flats or the white, terracotta-roofed villas which one finds in Jewish urban developments in Galilee. I drove up into this area one September afternoon. Arab music wafted in at the window from time to time as we passed a café or garage. By the side of the road lay several rusting cars, one abandoned old fridge, and much more garbage. I became so immersed in the feeling that I was in the Arab world that I was brought back to reality with a start by the sight of an Israeli flag flying over a police station. It looked totally out of place. It was the same shock that I had experienced driving around southern Lebanon at the time of the Israeli occupation and suddenly seeing there the flag of the Jewish state – the white and blue and the Star of David seem incongruous in any Arab setting. For all the evidence to the contrary in the form of identity cards, passports and voting rights, this part of Israel, these communities, can never be an integral part of the state of Israel in emotional and spiritual terms.

The small town of Ibilin (population about 7,000, both Muslims and Christians) is situated in the rolling hills north-east of Haifa and far enough away from the choking smog of that city for the air to be clear. Most of the town lies on a single hill which is dominated by a mosque with a thin minaret. Turning off the main road towards Ibilin, I was struck by the similarity between the scenery here and that in southern Lebanon, with its pastureland and olive groves. I was struck too by the change from order to disorder, from the generally clean streets and well paved highways of Jewish towns to the unkempt roadways, by half-finished houses and rubbish liberally strewn about the place. Children appeared wearing scruffy clothes; not all were wearing shoes. As I drove into the town I noticed how many walls had been daubed with Palestinian nationalist graffiti and the colours of the Palestinian flag, most of it crudely blotted out by black paint. The appearance of a foreigner in an Israeli-registered hire-car which was making its way nervously round the winding and narrow streets of Ibilin brought people to doorways to have a look. Their eyes spelt out unmistakable messages of distrust, even of hostility, reminiscent of what I encountered both in villages in the occupied West Bank, after the start of the Intifada, and in villages in southern Lebanon during the Israeli occupation – at the time of the Iron Fist policy conducted against the Shiite Lebanese population in 1984. When I found the person I'd come to see, the suspicion evaporated and was replaced by overwhelming hospitality.

Izzat Daoud, known as Abu Taufiq, is one of the elder statesmen of Ibilin. He stayed on in 1948, while some of his family went to Lebanon assuming it would be just for a matter of weeks before they would be able to return. They are still in Lebanon. At that time his sister went to Damascus, and now has a son living in Germany. Other members of his family live in the Ivory Coast, Canada and France. This is typical of tens of thousands of stories you hear from Palestinian families around the world. 'We're just like the Jews used to be before Israel [was created],' Abu Taufiq told me, going on to say how much of his land had been confiscated, how the economic problems in Israel were hitting the Arab communities hard, how the local branch of the Israeli bank was foreclosing on debts – a policy which had led the local Arab manager to resign in protest. 'The opportunities for Arabs are not as good as for Jews. We get less funds, and we don't get money from the Jewish Agency. Also all members of a Jewish family go out to work. This is not our tradition. It's not our tradition to allow, say a daughter to go to a factory to work at midnight.'

Their links with the Palestinian family world-wide and with its social and cultural traditions are striking. In one house a black-and-white photograph, hanging on a wall, showed a young man with a serious, business-like expression. Perhaps a passport photo enlarged. It was the cousin of my young host, who had been killed in the massacre of Palestinians at the Chatila refugee camp in Lebanon in 1982. My host was studying at the Hebrew University of Jerusalem at the time of Israel's war in Lebanon. He remembers a Jewish student knocking on his door one day and coming in to boast that he'd just come back from 'killing Palestinians' near the Litani River in Lebanon. That Jewish student is now a leading right-wing politician in Israel. Gaps are not closing. Is it any wonder?

From the roof of that same house I was shown the Jewish developments that had been built around this group of Arab towns and villages. And I saw a new road being laid which would take the inhabitants of one of the new Jewish towns directly to their doorsteps without the inconvenience (and the possible unpleasantness) of passing through Arab villages – never mind that the road had sliced through an olive grove outside Ibilin. 'They want to Judaize Galilee,' one of the men present said, gloomily. 'They're confiscating the land around their new settlements. Policies and finance are geared to the Jewish [and he stressed that word] state. Jews who come from abroad immediately get financial support. Our municipalities get less than their municipalities. They don't help us at all.'

Quite simply, the Arab municipalities do not have enough money to keep their towns and villages clean, nor to provide amenities that are anything close to those on offer to people living in Jewish communities. The Galilee Society for Health, Research and Services pointed out that among 'seventy-five recognized Arab villages in the region, with a total population of roughly 300,000, only five have functioning sewage systems. The other seventy (not to mention the unrecognized settlements) rely on the use of cesspits to percolate the sewage into the soil where it would be filtered. However, the substratum of porous limestone with a thin layer of topsoil, common throughout Galilee, has proven to be inappropriate for filtration. The sewage readily infiltrates the water-table, contaminating local wells and springs at the same time that it saturates the soil in which lie the drinking-water pipes. This facilitates their early corrosion and causes water losses as high as forty per cent in some villages.'

The difference between the standards of basic facilities available each to Arab and Jewish communities is obvious. The evidence is not secret, it is available in government statistics. Dr Alex Bligh, the deputy adviser to the Prime Minister on Arab Affairs, said in a background paper published in May 1990 that the level of services in Arab settlements had 'risen greatly since the beginning of the 1960s. However, because the initial level of development in these settlements was lower than that of Jewish settlements, there is still a large gap between the two sectors.' More difficult to quantify is the difference in opportunities available. It all begins in school.

George Kanazi is more fortunate than many Arab Israelis because he lives in a large family house on the edge of Nazareth, and his book-lined study is set apart from the noises of the home. He is notable in one other important respect too: he's the first Israeli Arab to become a professor in an Israeli university. The fact that in a period of forty years and more this section of the Israeli population (seventeen or eighteen per cent of the total) has produced only one university professor is a clear sign of different educational standards. 'The gap is very evident to us,' Professor Kanazi told me, 'to people who work at the university.'

There are practical problems right from the start. Shukri Abed is an Israeli Arab attached to the Truman Institute for the advancement of peace at the Hebrew University of Jerusalem. 'We're always complaining about the shortage of classrooms in Arab schools. Take a village like

Umm el-Fahm, for example, where they had to rent rooms from private houses.' He sees the 'deliberate policy' of the government in underfunding Arab education as part of the problem, but only part: 'I don't think I would blame it entirely on the Jewish authorities. I mean, there's the whole structure of our villages, for example, the lack of education facilities and the entire atmosphere of "non-education."'

When the state of Israel was created, standards of education among the Arab community were low, the rate of illiteracy was high. A decision was taken then to allow the Arab community to continue its own education system in its own language. A common answer from Israelis to Arab complaints about the inadequacies of their education is one to the effect that they should be grateful, as one commentator put it, 'to the attitude of liberal magnanimity' which allowed them to continue classes in Arabic rather than in Hebrew. And there is the undeniable fact that the level of education among the Israeli Arabs has risen enormously over the past forty years. To quote, once again, Dr Alex Bligh from the Arab Affairs department at the Prime Minister's office: 'In the field of education, the Arab community in Israel has undergone a veritable revolution. . . . At the time of the establishment of the state, about 11,000 [Arab] students studied in the state educational system. In 1988, that number stood at 240,000, i.e. an increase of more than twenty-fold.' The retort to these answers was given by Mohammed Habib Allah, of the National Committee of Leaders of Arab Councils: 'We don't compare ourselves to how we were forty years ago, or to Arabs in other countries. We compare ourselves to the rest of the citizens of Israel.' And by that standard, the Arabs fall well short of the Jews.

The school curriculum is tightly controlled by the Ministry of Education, within which is an Arab Department headed by Arabs who, according to Shukri Abed, 'have sold their souls to Israel. And they are totally unrespected by Arabs.' While in mathematics and the science subjects there is no great difference between the Arab and Jewish curricula, the teaching of history and literature within Arab schools is selective, to say the least. Arab teachers I spoke to said children learn nothing about the golden age of the Arab empire and its contribution to Western culture: the emphasis is on Jewish history, and any reference to Arab (and especially Palestinian) nationalism is proscribed. The events of 1948 and the 'departure' of hundreds of thousands of Palestinians, for example, are taught entirely from the Jewish perspective. In the view of

Khaula Abu Bakr, educational counsellor from Acre: 'In the educational system they must learn to be more Israeli, and not Arab or Palestinian. And to be an Israeli is to learn what Israel as a state is doing for the benefit of Arabs and Jews. Programmes in schools have nothing to do with Arab culture or Arab history, or with the political identity of Arabs either now or before 1948. They are trying to cover up that part totally. They are trying to teach them to be "good Arabs" which means "good Israelis". The aim is to demolish the Palestinian Arab identity. I don't believe that a person can be healthy in his own mental health if he doesn't respect his own identity. So we're trying to teach them at home what it is being an Arab and a Palestinian. What the educational system isn't giving them, I and other parents and Palestinian organizations are trying to give them.'

Professor Kanazi, the first Arab professor in Israel, feels equally strongly: 'I believe that all attempts to suppress identity were doomed to failure a long time before the Intifada. The sense of identity has grown and shifted towards strengthening the Palestinian factor, and the fact that Palestinian literature was not taught and is not taught at our schools doesn't prevent people from reading. We have radios, Arab countries around us, we have books and magazines. And this has made the schools look as if they're far away from the practical scenery of every individual. And this is a failure, in fact.'

Khaula Abu Bakr believes that 'the gap between Arab and Jewish education is about twenty years. If we wanted to get equal we'd have to stop the Jewish system for twenty years and give all the resources to the Arab system for twenty years. Of all elementary-school pupils in Israel, twenty-three per cent are Arabs; among university students, the figure is six per cent, with a high drop-out rate. Often a student from a traditional, sheltered, Arabic-cultured background finds that he can't bridge the gap to his Jewish contemporaries from a more liberal background, who are more worldly-wise having just completed three years of army service.'

Another obstacle facing young Arabs who want to go to university is language. While most will be able to converse in Hebrew, their written knowledge is often inadequate. Shukri Abed highlights this as a major problem. 'I can see when I grade exams that the Arabs probably know what they want to write but can't express it. You know, I just feel so sorry for that. So I gave them the choice of writing in Arabic, but unfortunately their Arabic is not very good either. In most cases I don't find it very illuminating to read their work — unlike some of the Jewish kids who study Islamic studies, for instance. The ones I teach are much, much better in understanding the material. Partly probably because they have a much more organized way of thinking, they've been trained that way.'

But even those Arabs who make it successfully through the education system face the problem of getting work. There's no comparison, Shukri Abed says, between what's available to Jews and to Arabs. 'What do we do? Most of us go to teach, in elementary or high schools. The few lucky ones among us go and teach in universities. But it's a very, very low percentage.' Shukri Abed has been trying without success for several years to get a permanent position at a university and believes that he and others are victims of a deliberate policy of keeping Arabs out of the top academic jobs for fear of the influence they would be able to exert, given the fact that the Arab community in Israel stands at around three-quarters of a million. There are other constraints, too. Many of the best engineering jobs, for example, are in industries which are related in some way to the army, and because of the security risk involved Arabs stand no chance whatsoever of getting them. The Centre for Jewish-Arab Economic Development reports that forty-two per cent of all Arab university graduates are either unemployed or under-employed, and that only one industrial zone has been designated in all the Arab settlements in the country. As one of the directors of the centre said: 'It's as if two states exist within the framework of one, a colonialistic relationship in which one exploits the labour resources of the other. It's not a healthy situation.'

In the final analysis, Arabs have to accept, by definition, the fact that they are not going to get the top positions in Israel. The arrival of hundreds of thousands of Soviet Jews in Israel, many of whom are highly qualified, led to competition within the job market becoming even more intense than before, and prominent members of Israel's Arab community expressed the fear that priority in employment would be given to the new arrivals and that more land would be confiscated from Arabs to house them.

The Israeli Arab from Ibilin who was at the Hebrew University told me what some of his Jewish contemporaries were doing now. Apart from the one member of the Knesset, another was a senior civil servant in the Ministry of Labour, and the rest had generally respectable jobs. He is a journalist and puts all his time and money into running a magazine for the Arab community. 'It's a little bit frustrating,' he told me. 'We Arabs have to grow up alone without any help [of the kind provided to the Jewish community]. If we emerge, we emerge like a plant from the desert.' He no longer has any link with his contemporaries from university, although he had recently by chance met the Knesset member, whom he quotes as saying: 'You're a writer. I'm not a writer. People write about me. But don't worry, we know everything about you.' High-profile Israeli Arabs, those regarded as potential trouble-makers, accept that their movements are carefully monitored by the authorities. They cite the fact that their backgrounds are much better known to the security services — and have been for more than forty years — than those of Palestinians in the Occupied Territories as another practical reason why any insurrection in Galilee would be almost certainly nipped in the bud.

Health care is one area where many Israeli Arabs find work, and some become surgeons. But again, academic or professional success doesn't completely bridge gaps. The following is an extract from an interview conducted with a successful Israeli Arab a year or two back by the *Jerusalem Post*: 'I have studied your language [Hebrew], your culture, I know the poems of Haim Nahman Bialik better than any Arab poet. I work here in an Israeli hospital, a respected surgeon, and yet I am a complete stranger to most of you. For all the doctors here, for all the patients, I am an Arab, and nothing will change this fact.'

This division between Jew and Arab is evident on some days more than others. In the aftermath of the 'Bus 405' attack in 1989, when a Palestinian from the occupied Gaza Strip forced a bus off the Tel Aviv to Jerusalem highway and down a ravine, killing and injuring many people, anger was translated from time to time into attacks on Israeli Arabs as well as Palestinians from the Occupied Territories. On the Saturday afternoon just after the incident three Israeli Arabs went to the beach at Caesarea for a swim. They were set upon and beaten by a group of Jewish Israelis, presumed to be members of the ultra right-wing racist movement, Kach. An Israel Radio reporter came on the scene a short time later. 'The Arab youth knelt on the beach bleeding. He was crying, "Please have mercy on me." Many bathers rushed to help, but when they noticed that the people being beaten were Arabs, many joined in with fists and sticks.'

The Israelis, in my opinion, have devised an almost perfect formula for alienating and radicalizing the substantial Arab community in their midst. They allow them to be citizens, yet keep them as outsiders by denying them the resources to develop the facilities they would need to take even the first step on the road towards equality. They expect the

Arabs to be loyal citizens of the Jewish state, and expect them to put their Palestinian and Arab identity into second place, without offering them a full Israeli identity in exchange. Teddy Kollek, who is wiser than many Israelis and has had more daily contact with Palestinians than most, made the following observation about the Arabs of East Jerusalem, the city which Israelis regard as the capital of the Jewish state. The Arabs of East Jerusalem are not Israeli citizens, but the observation is nonetheless valid: 'The Arab community in Jerusalem cannot be bought by more and better schools, more and better roads. But we could have avoided some of the feeling of economic discrimination which has only added to the feelings of national discrimination.'

So much for the policy of economic discrimination. As for the policy of doctoring the school curriculum to eliminate evidence of Palestinian and Arab nationalism, it is hard to disagree with George Kanazi, the first Arab professor at an Israeli university: 'Pressure creates reaction; the more you're pressed, the more you ask questions about your identity. And this continuous pressure over the past forty years has brought about the awakening of the Palestinian identity.'

The sword which hangs over the heads of the Arabs of Israel is the certainty that if their loyalty to the state is found wanting to any serious degree, the call from voices on the right wing for their suppression and even their expulsion would be loud and persuasive. ('No countries in the real world . . . are ready to waste any sympathy on the fate of minorities which are adjudged to be hostile to the majority – all the more so when such hostility is evinced in the midst of a protracted war,' one political commentator wrote after the riots in Nazareth in May 1990.) And in the short term there appear to be no prospects of an Israeli government taking steps to remove inequality between Jews and Arabs. Professor Arnon Soffer from the Department of Geography and Social Sciences at Haifa University puts it this way: 'Whoever deludes himself into thinking that it's still possible to solve the problem of Galilee Arabs through money and sewer systems is simply living in a dream world. Until the first Arab pilot serves in the Israeli air force – and we know that this will never happen – they will continue to shout about discrimination. The increasing signs of nationalism point to a process which we can't stop.'

But that prediction was made before the unexpected wave of Jewish immigration from the Soviet Union. Without this influx, Professor Soffer says, by the end of the century the Arabs would have accounted for twenty-two per cent of the Israeli population, with more than a million Arabs living in the Galilee area and fostering hopes of autonomy and nationalism. But he believes that if, as predicted, up to one million more Jews come to Israel, many 'by seepage' will eventually settle in Galilee, so that it will be 'a mixed society there with no more talk of autonomy and irredentism'.

Aside from demographic considerations there is still the question of the basic distrust of Arabs which, as we have seen throughout this book, lies somewhere — to a greater or lesser extent — in the minds of many Israelis. On these grounds alone Dr Ilan Pappe, a specialist on Arab affairs at Haifa University, rules out the possibility of an end to discrimination against the Arabs. He points to the fact that for the first twenty years of Israel's existence Arabs were governed by a military regime. 'What we have is an Israeli fear, a belief that it's better to discriminate in some way against the Arabs of Israel in order not to endanger the security of the country; and I think it's really a matter of self-confidence. As long as Israelis will not feel secure vis-à-vis the Arabs in Israel or the Arabs in general, I don't think we will see a pluralistic or purely democratic state in Israel. The Arab minority would always, I think, suffer from some sort of discrimination.'

Discrimination against Arabs has become endemic in the daily life of Israel. It is accepted that Arabs from the Occupied Territories will do the hard and unpleasant work which Jewish Israelis have little inclination to take on — the kind of work done by Pakistanis or Indians in the Gulf States. When the Intifada began to cause disruptions to the flow of cheap labour from the Occupied Territories, the first inclination of Israeli employers was to seek exemptions from the immigration authorities to allow labourers to be brought in from Turkey and other countries in the region.

Unlike the Palestinians in the Occupied Territories, those inside Israel have the theoretical power to improve their position through the ballot box. But the Arab vote has always been fragmented. Both the communists and the Israeli Labour party, along with smaller groups, attract its support, and prevent any effective Arab bloc being created. Also, with a variety of political opinions found among the Arab community, the creation of a united platform would not be easy. Abdel Wahab Darawshe used to be a Knesset member representing the Labour party. Before the 1988 general election he resigned in protest at the actions of the Israeli army in the Occupied Territories, and formed the Arab Democratic Party. At his office in Nazareth he told me how in the past the Arabs had wasted their votes, 'More than thirty per cent didn't even cast a vote. Of those who did, some forty per cent voted for Jewish parties. So the result is that we have six rather than sixteen Arab members of the Knesset.'

What would happen if there were a solid Arab bloc of fifteen or sixteen seats in the Knesset, holding the balance of power between Labour and Likud? Most Arab and Jewish commentators I consulted believed that if this looked likely, the system would be changed to prevent it happening.

Arabs complain also that there is an attempt by the Israelis to isolate the various communities within them – as one leading figure put it, 'to divide and rule, to weaken us. To deal with us as minorities, as religious minorities.' For example, special Israeli attention is given to fostering interest within the Arab Druze community (about 17,000 strong) in their own heritage. Since the mid-1950s Druze men have been obliged to serve in the Israeli army; their tough behaviour towards Palestinians in the Occupied Territories has caused resentment among the majority Arab Israeli community. Arab Bedouin are also a separate category. Some of them serve in the army, even though they are not obliged to, which again is a source of irritation and division.

For the overwhelming majority of Israeli Arabs the problem of daily life comes down to striking a balance between the struggle for equality in Israel and an increasing identity with Palestinian nationalism. One option is to leave the country, but most Israeli Arabs I've met (and opinion polls back this up) want to stay on their land, and would continue to stay even if a Palestinian state were to be created in the West Bank and Gaza Strip. The other clear fact, though, is that the secular leadership of the Arab Israeli community has failed to make headway in the battle for social and economic equality; nor is it likely that much more headway will be made in the foreseeable future, given the entrenched attitudes of the Israelis. This is the Middle East. At times of frustration and despair, as we have noted several times, religion is a great comfort – so in Egypt, so in Lebanon, so in Jordan, and so in Muslim communities inside Israel. In municipal elections which followed the 1988 general election, Islamic groups did surprisingly well in a number of towns. Their tactics have been no different from those of the Islamic fundamentalists in upper Egypt or the Jewish fundamentalists in the development towns in

Israel.

Dr Rafi Israeli of the Hebrew University of Jerusalem has made a study of these developments: 'Islamic groups within Arab Israeli society are gaining strength, there's no doubt. It's exactly the same process as in Jordan and the Occupied Territories. The more the nationalist element is losing ground – and it is – the more the Muslim element is gaining. The Communist party had promised the Israeli Arabs for years that if they followed it it would bring about equality in services, and so on. And the communists did nothing about it and so lost out completely. The religious parties succeeded, not because of their promises but because of their actions: they did what they'd undertaken to do [as mentioned in the previous chapter] – they built schools, and they built clinics and they built roads, and so on. They are following the example of the Muslim brotherhood in Egypt and Hamas [the Islamic resistance movement] in the territories.'

Surely, then, the case for eliminating economic and social inequalities between Jews and Arabs in Israel is beyond challenge if the drift towards fundamentalism is to be checked? Dr Rafi Israeli doesn't agree. 'I heard one of the Arab leaders a few years ago, with the rise of fundamentalism, say: "Now that our stomachs are full we have to address ourselves to our spiritual, emotional and national problems." For me that's a very significant statement . . . If it were a matter of economics, then they [the Israeli Arabs] might say they were an ethnic, religious group which is kept behind because of the lack of Israeli funds, and so on. However, for the past ten years they've been saying: "We are no longer an ethnic, linguistic, religious minority, we are a national minority, and that means we live in a bi-national state." That has a totally different significance from a disadvantaged group, because there are other disadvantaged groups in Israel, those who live in slums, the Sephardi people and all that. But they don't say they live in a bi-national state – where there's a state of the Ashkenazim and their own.'

What worries Dr Israeli even more is that the Arab community within the Jewish state has not only assimilated the religious currents in the region but has also absorbed the radically anti-Israeli spirit mixed up in them. 'The quotations from their publications make your hair stand on end. Not only are they calling [like Hamas in the Territories] for the overthrow of the state of Israel, but they're also repeating the anti-Jewish stereotypes about the greed, expansionism of Jews, about how they are ruling the world and world media – all the things that we thought had disappeared are reappearing here. In my mind it's becoming very dangerous and very explosive.'

All this leaves the Christian Arab community in Israel feeling a little uncomfortable. Islamic fundamentalism is not a driving force throughout the Muslim Arab community in Israel, any more than it is in Jordan or Egypt. But it has definitely established its credentials. If the trend continues, then Christian Arabs will most likely find themselves pushed into increasingly radical positions within the secular nationalist movement to prove that they are no less loyal to the Palestinian and Arab cause than their Muslim brethren.

Israel has a problem on its hands. I think that Dr Rafi Israeli is right when he says there are 'clear signs that things are getting out of hand'. It's true in almost every country in the region. In the absence of a peace process, in the absence of hope that economic conditions will improve, and in the absence of a secular political system that largely commands the respect of the population, there will be a revival in religious observation – call it 'fundamentalism' or not. Nothing underlines more clearly Israel's inextricable link with the Middle East than the developments within its own Arab community. Despite the restrictions placed upon it (and I would argue it's in no small part because of their imposition), the Israeli authorities have not been able to stop the forging of bonds with the Arabs outside. Since they hold Israeli passports, Arabs in the Jewish state can visit easily only one other country in the region: Egypt (although since 1978 a quota of Muslims has been allowed to pass through Jordan to Saudi Arabia each year to perform the pilgrimage to Mecca). Therefore Israeli Arabs feel isolated, cut off from the mainstream of the Arab world. But this isolation is evaporating as religious and nationalist bonds are strengthening – in large part because of the Intifada. Since 1973 the stigma attached to Israeli Arabs in the eyes of those elsewhere has gradually been obliterated, and since that time there have been frequent contacts between prominent Israeli Arabs and leaders of the PLO outside the country. It has become a common sight to see Arab members of the Knesset taking part in nationalist-inspired protests in East Jerusalem and the Occupied Territories.

This is a problem for Israel, because as long as the loyalty of the Arabs is not open to serious question, as long as they work within the system (albeit, as in the case of the Islamic fundamentalist groups, exploiting it for their own goals), then the authorities will not be able to adopt a clear policy towards them. I believe that the phenomenon of the Israeli Arabs (taken in conjunction with developments within the Sephardi community) has forced Israel to face the reality of life in the Middle East. This has not increased Israel's sympathy with the Arabs and their aspirations — quite the reverse. A vision of 'an enemy within' working quietly behind the scenes is enough to feed Israeli paranoia and increase the Israelis' distrust of Arabs as a whole. Government ministers warn about the dangers of Israeli Arabs becoming radicalized. An old-time Israeli, secular and left-wing in his outlook, reflected on the rise of Islamic fundamentalism: 'This is a very big problem for us — to live very near and to be overshadowed by this phenomenon. Fundamentalism is turning the clock back, and even the most active politicians don't pay enough attention to it. It frightens me when I see the penetration of those ideas in the Arab population of Israel, the influence of Hamas in their mosques. I can't help thinking this is a step back in the quest for co-existence.'

The problem is that the 'quest for co-existence' was conducted along lines which were never going to grant the Arabs equal rights and which depended on keeping them both at arm's length and under the thumb. A united Arab Israeli community — united by fundamentalism or radical Palestinian nationalism — would be unacceptable. The identification of Israeli Arabs with the aspirations of the inhabitants of the West Bank and the Gaza Strip is deep-rooted. Until and unless a solution is found to that problem, the Israeli Arabs will continue to feel their loyalties torn, and will become increasingly radicalized. Despite what some right-wing Israelis say, the Arabs of Israel are not 'the enemy within'. At least, not yet. If that day comes, I believe that Israel will have little choice but to deal with these stark Middle East phenomena with stark Middle East methods.

But an equally awkward dilemma would face an Israeli government on the day when, and if, a peace settlement for the region were finally reached. The authorities would then have to face the wrath of Israel's new pioneers, those who for the past few decades have been strengthening the outer defences of the fortress state by settling the territories captured (but not incorporated into Israel) in the 1967 Middle East War: the Jewish settlers in the Occupied Territories.

—————————— •◆• ——————————

CHAPTER TEN

New battlements, new battles?

O N a sunbaked, barren ridge in the dusty Judean hills east of
Jerusalem, at the end of May 1990, the construction of the latest
Jewish settlement in the occupied West Bank was newly under
way. Gady Buiumsohn, a young Israeli who has spent most of his life in
the United States, was one of those helping to set up the first temporary
accommodation at Allon. He was quite clear about his motives for
moving to the Occupied Territories: 'We have every right to be in these
areas, and the right comes from the Bible. One of the reasons that I came
here at this particular time was to be a slap in the face to the Arab rioters
who believe that every stone they throw is turning away another Jew. We
believe that every stone they throw is bringing another Jew here.'

Rabbi Dov Berkovits has had much more experience than Gady
Buiumsohn of living in the Territories. He has been a member of the
settlement of Shilo, situated in the hills between Ramallah and Nablus in
the West Bank, for ten years. 'I never expected to live in an area where
people around you want you out and despise you – I think to a certain
extent hate you, many of them, not all of them. I think it's only made me
feel much more strongly the necessity and importance for the Jewish
people to be living here.'

The Occupied Territories are the new front line; this is where the
psychological war of the Middle East has been fought since June 1967
when the Israeli army defeated the Jordanians in the West Bank and the
Egyptians in the Gaza Strip. From time to time, and especially since the
start of the Intifada in December 1987, the war of nerves has erupted into
violence perpetrated by individuals and groups on both sides. It is the key
battleground, because these territories are the prize sought by both sides.
For the majority of Palestinians, the withdrawal of the Israeli army from

the Occupied Territories and Arab East Jerusalem is a minimal requirement: hardliners, secular and religious, see this as the first step towards the eventual elimination of Israel. The voices of those Palestinians who believe a compromise over territory is possible are being drowned by increasing clamour, and similar voices on the Israeli side have equal difficulty in making themselves heard. Many Israelis believe the Territories should remain under their control, without being incorporated into the Jewish state; but hardliners say the Territories are already, *de facto*, part of Israel and will always be such, as the quotes at the start of this chapter made clear. Thus the existence of the Jewish settlements and their future fate are crucial elements in the Middle East conflict.

The word 'settlement' is imprecise and often misleading. In Hebrew the word used is 'yishuv' which means both settlement and 'community'. But more often than not these Jewish outposts would be more accurately labelled towns or villages – indeed many settlers refer to them as such. In short, 'settlement' implies a state of impermanence, but while the outside world may talk about Jewish settlements as objects which one day might be conveniently removed as part of some future peace package, the Jewish settlements in the Occupied Territories have been built to last. Many of them (like Ma'ale Adumim east of Jerusalem) are dense and sprawling satellite suburbs, or (like Ariel or Elkana to the east of Tel Aviv) are dormitory towns for the major cities. Some Israelis are undoubtedly attracted to the West Bank by little more than the comparatively low cost of property, and do not necessarily have strong Zionist or religious motives for living there. But the main core of settlers is ideologically motivated.

'Zionism was here but it was expelled,' Amos Oz writes in his book, *In the Land of Israel,* after visiting a formerly mixed secular-religious neighbourhood of Jerusalem that had been taken over by ultra-orthodox Jews. To find Zionism today, and more particularly Zionism motivated by strong religious convictions, you have to travel to the settlements in the occupied West Bank and Gaza Strip where between 60,000 and 70,000 Israelis have their homes.

The seven p.m. bus to Shilo thundered through the Arab suburbs of north Jerusalem, with Nancy and Frank Sinatra singing 'Somethin' Stupid' on the radio. Like all the buses which travel into the Occupied Territories it bore the marks of the conflict there – several of the windows had been hit by rocks, but a plastic coating had stopped the glass breaking, leaving instead a number of many-legged-spider patterns. The bus was about half full; all the men, including two soldiers with their M-16 assault rifles, wore knitted kippas, the hallmark of the settlers. Many had beards, many had pistols tucked into their trouser waistbands. In a seat slightly ahead and to the right of me, a bearded man cradled the bus's fire-extinguisher on his lap all the way to Shilo. He remembered the petrol-bomb attack on a bus passing through Jericho in October 1988, in which a mother and her three young children were killed, and he reckoned that if a petrol bomb somehow ignited inside this particular vehicle there wouldn't be time to reach down and unstrap its extinguisher.

My companion on the bus gave me a running commentary on well-known trouble spots as we headed out of the city. 'This we call the corner of the green mosque, we sometimes get hit here.' 'This is Al-Amari refugee camp.' Do they get stoned from there? 'Sometimes.' 'The village coming up often gives us trouble – and sometimes along here we get hit by stones thrown down from the hill above.' 'Just over here a family driving out of Shilo were attacked by a petrol bomb – it smashed the windshield, but it didn't explode.'

When settlers find their vehicles coming under attack they often get out and chase the stone-throwers; sometimes Palestinians are beaten up or shot, which draws criticism from within Israel as well as from the outside world. My companion explained the settlers' view: 'We're not acting as vigilantes, but when stones are thrown at you, you're aware that your neighbour or your family will also be going past that same spot, and you feel responsible for them. If you have the opportunity to clean up the area, you do. You fire a few shots and chase them. We get accused of over-reaction. But being in the place we are we have a heightened sense of responsibility for others, and it just comes out this way.'

Shilo, situated on three adjoining hilltops, looked like a quiet country town in the soft dusk, with lights from the surrounding Arab villages and Jewish settlements beginning to sparkle. When the bus had departed I was struck by the breathless silence and the sense of calm. It felt every bit like a remote outpost, under the half-moon and the early evening stars. A little later I recognized some of the men who had been on the bus congregating for evening prayers in the synagogue, a sparse Portakabin lit by neon strips and bare bulbs. Pinned on a board outside was the rota for guard duty – at the school during the morning, and during both day and night at the gate to the settlement.

To my surprise, Shilo (unlike some other settlements) is not surrounded by a security fence; at night arc lights at regular intervals mark the five-mile circumference. Whether or not to build a fence is a subject of debate among the 100 families (195 adults and 380 children) of Shilo, and is another element in the war of nerves between the Jewish and Palestinian communities. For despite the frequent attacks on vehicles on the roads close to Shilo, the settlement itself has never been touched. And while some settlers at Shilo argue that a fence is an essential precaution, given the hostility in neighbouring villages, one lady explained the contrary and majority view: 'If we feel that this land belongs to us, then there's no reason to have a fence. Of course we have guards and you have to be careful. But the moment you fence a place off it means you're scared and the people who live on the other side of the fence are your enemies. And then you have a problem explaining it to your children. They'd say: "This is your country, why are you fencing it off?"'

The Intifada has seen a marked worsening in relations between Palestinians in the Occupied Territories and the Jewish settlers, but not all contacts have been broken off. While I was in Shilo I saw a car with Arab West Bank number plates and with three Palestinian men in it, driving into the settlement. Some Palestinians are still employed there each day – mainly on construction work. And the biggest construction project under way while I was visiting Shilo was the new central synagogue, built with angular pillars and a flat roof, as a large-scale replica of the ancient Jewish Tabernacle which contained the Ark of the Covenant and which stayed in Shilo for 369 years during a period shortly after the Exodus from Egypt.

'And the whole congregation of the children of Israel assembled together at Shiloh and set up the tabernacle of the congregation there. And the land was subdued before them.' – Joshua, Chapter 10.

Indeed, it was on the pretext of setting up an archaeological encampment that the first Jewish settlers came to Shilo in 1978, during a difficult phase in the peace negotiations, brokered by President Carter, between Egypt and Israel. The affair angered Egypt and threatened to cause a breakdown in the negotiations. President Carter was annoyed too: 'I deeply regret the effort to establish another illegal settlement on the West Bank at Shilo. However, I'm confident that Prime Minister Begin will honour the commitment made to me, and thus will not allow this settlement to go ahead.'

The fact that it did go ahead and that the land was duly 'subdued before them' once more says a lot about the determination of the settlers and the support they have received from successive governments. The building of settlements after 1967 began under Labour and was accelerated when Likud came to power. The majority were created by the World Zionist Organization and the Israeli Ministry of Housing, with money coming from the government's purse. The purchase of the land and the planning and preparation of the infrastructure are the responsibility of the Jewish National Fund. Outside official circles, Gush Emunim ('Bloc of the Faithful', a religious Zionist movement created in 1974) has led aggressive efforts to establish new settlements – sometimes with prior government approval, sometimes without it – in order to establish Jewish sovereignty over the land, and to organize and co-ordinate the settlers' position on matters of politics and security.

Shilo, with its white-painted villas with sloping tiled roofs, has an air of calm and relaxation which belies the 'Wild West' image that many Israelis – not to mention people outside Israel – have about settlement life. Everyone I spoke to was enthusiastic about the lifestyle and about the stunning beauty of the surrounding hills and valleys. Within the settlement the atmosphere is not unlike that of a kibbutz, with a strong sense of community. People leave their doors unlocked, children's bicycles lie on the patches of grass between the houses. There are no fences inside Shilo any more than there is one around the outside of the settlement. In the morning the children scamper unaccompanied down the hillside to the school which serves Shilo and two other settlements. Settlers insist that while the headlines are made by a handful from among their community who are vociferous in their militancy, the 'silent majority' is simply trying to lead a normal life. 'What you see on TV are the little wars in the Arab cities,' Yeshua De'haan, the young mayor of Shilo said. 'This is not like a war zone. We lead a regular life. Yes, there are some problems on the roads, but that doesn't make it all into a major problem. The most important thing is that we live here, we like to live here and we like to live in peace and quiet.' Even the 'problems on the roads' have lessened since the installation of shatterproof windows on all buses and cars used by the settlers. This simple invention has removed much of the anxiety from settlers' lives; especially considering the fact that their children sometimes have to travel many miles to school by bus each day.

This attitude of contentment and confidence is fine, of course, provided that one ducks two pressing questions; should the settlers be in the Territories in the first place, given the widely held international view often expressed by the United States that settlement activity on land under military occupation is illegal and an obstacle to peace? And secondly, what about the demands of the Palestinians?

Settlers, for the most part, like other right-wing Israelis, handle the second question by refusing to recognize the existence of Palestinian nationalism. In the view of Gady Buiumsohn from Allon, 'the so-called Palestinians already have a state: Jordan. They want to own this land, not because it's important to them, it's not; they want it only because we've come here. Before the state of Israel was created the Arabs did nothing here.'

At Shilo I asked Batya Medad, who came originally from the United States and is the mother of five children, how she could deny the existence of Palestinian nationalism – she might not like it, but surely it had to be addressed? 'We don't have to respect it, because it's a joke compared with Jewish feelings and Jewish attachment to this land. We're talking about Jewish people who've lived on this land through thousands of years. Palestinian nationalism is a modern thing, it never existed – and it's a big sham, a big fakery. The Palestinians are a group of people. This land was an empty space, a crossroads. No other people except the Jews ever had a nation based in this area. Jerusalem was only ever the capital of the Jewish nation, of no other. The PLO's public relations campaign has been excellent, but it's a sham.'

Some settlers, followers of Meir Kahane's anti-Arab Kach movement, say the only answer is to expel all the Arabs from the Territories. Most settlers with whom I have spoken said they were prepared to let Palestinians stay in the West Bank and Gaza Strip, provided that they dropped their nationalistic claims and remained peaceful; in other words, on terms dictated by the settlers themselves. Most I spoke to also were convinced beyond a shadow of doubt (though without being able to prove it) that the majority of Palestinians wanted to live at peace with the Jews, but were being terrorized by the PLO. Most, too, thought that the army should take tougher action against troublemakers and expel all PLO-backed leaders of the Intifada. But could there be any co-existence on this battlefield of the Middle East conflict? I very much doubt it. When one talks to Palestinians or other Arabs it doesn't take long to discover a deep-rooted hatred and distrust of 'the Jews', as the Israelis are usually described.

The distrust is shared from the other side. Still in Shilo, Rifka Marantz, mother of five children with a sixth expected, said she tried to teach her family about the need for co-existence. 'When we talk about what happens with the Arabs we talk as we would about our own people – the same way you have good Jews and bad Jews, so you have good Arabs and bad Arabs. The children know that if an Arab plants a bomb in some place it doesn't mean that everyone will do the same. That's the kind of attitude I try to give over to my children – that not every Arab is bad. But I'm not saying one should trust them. One can never be sure.' I asked Rabbi Dov Berkovits if he thought there was room for two peoples in the West Bank. 'I once thought so, I don't think so now...I think right now it's either them or me, them or us.' And it was at that point that Rabbi Berkovits expressed his conviction that it was more essential than ever for him and for all the other Jews in the Occupied Territories not to leave.

So the settlers themselves are absolutely convinced of their right to be on the land, and are equally determined to stay, despite the opposition of the local Arab population and the Arabs as a whole. But they also have to counter the opposition from inside Israel and from the international community. As Israelis as a whole believe they are not reported fairly by the international media, so settlers are of the view that their case is misrepresented by a generally hostile press inside the Jewish state. Yisrael Medad, an official with the right-wing Tehiya party and a resident of Shilo, says the result is that settlers take a defensive attitude. 'Reporters are classified as an interference, something to be avoided.' Rifka Marantz believes that, 'the newspapers here unfortunately are not on our side. I think the trouble with a lot of Israelis is that they're naive and feel that if an Arab says "We want peace, we want peace," he really means it. But we don't think so. They're really looking to throw us out.'

Rabbi Berkovits says international pressure from the United States and the Soviet Union amounts to nothing more than 'political self-interest and cynicism. The problem that really bothers me is the attitude that many Israelis have towards settlements. And I see it as a question which sometimes gives me concern – if push comes to shove, as it may very soon, will the government be willing to defend me?'

Settlers are the new Zionists, the new breed of idealists who wear their idealism on their sleeves at a time when Zionist idealism within Israel has waned. This fact alone, in the opinion of Rabbi Berkovits, makes settlers unpopular with many Israelis. 'I think it's very unfortunate, but I think it's true. It's one reason why so many Israelis find us a thorn in their sides – because they don't want to see the flag of Zionism. They don't want to see their own failures reflected in the fact that the flag is in our hand, not the hands of the left, not the secular socialists, but the right and religious idealists. I think all this causes a lot of people bad nights.'

As we have seen in earlier chapters, the coming-of-age of the Jewish state has been accompanied by a decline in the fortunes of the secular, pioneering Zionists and a corresponding drift towards materialism – and religion. Religious Israelis say the secular Zionists established the roots of the Jewish state and set up the machinery for the ingathering of the exiles. But once Jewish people left their ghettoes around the world and came into contact with Jewish land, it was inevitable – they continue – that Judaism would flower again. What the settlers say is that Zionism must flower again too. They blame on the long years of Labour rule the fact that the education system in the Jewish state has failed to inculcate new generations of Israelis with the ideals of Zionism.

Batya Medad feels strongly about this, and believes that proof of Labour's bankrupt ideology is the fact that they've 'lost their children'. The offspring of the big names in Labour – of Golda Meir, Shimon Peres, Yitzhak Rabin, and so on – have not followed in their parents' footsteps, and there is no young and dynamic leadership on the left to match that on the right or within the religious community. The fact is, she continued, that 'nationalist' leaders have been more successful in 'holding on to' their children because they have taught them Zionism in their homes.

Batya Medad believes that the fault lies in the school curriculum, in the 'wishy-washy' teaching of history which has failed to spell out 'why we're here as Jews, why we should have no doubts. The history of our people and the history of Zionism are not taught in such a way as to instil patriotism. We don't have to apologize for existing and defending our land. Labour tried to make us people of the world instead of Jews, always concerned that the goyim should like us. That attitude was based on a ghetto mentality. We've nothing to be ashamed of, we're not the aggressors, we've been the ones attacked in all the wars. So we won, what's the crime? I really don't care what any other countries think. My own people come first. And the more pronouncements that come from the United States, the more radical I get. The problem is that Israel is so apologetic. We should tell the US to go to hell.'

One of Batya's daughters is just finishing school. I asked her if she planned to travel abroad after her two years' army duty, in the footsteps of thousands of young Israelis. No, she said, many Israelis went away to try to find themselves, to seek a spiritual identity. 'But I'm religious. I don't need that, I have it all here' – and she pointed to the hills outside their house. Her ambitions reflect her religious Zionist upbringing. After the army she wants to study, then get married and have seven, eight or nine children. If there are still difficulties in the Occupied Territories she plans to remain in Shilo to do her bit towards keeping the land in Jewish hands. Otherwise she'd like to go to Galilee to help redress the demographic imbalance there, which is weighted towards the Arabs.

A population explosion is around the corner among the new Zionists. Large families are the order of the day. Around half the population of Jews living in the Occupied Territories still have children at high school and the next few years will see them marrying and carrying on the tradition of large families. Then there is the whole question of the Soviet immigrants. Arab countries have raised a furore over the possibility of tens of thousands of Soviet Jews being settled in the Occupied Territories, thus greatly strengthening Jewish control of the land. The Soviet Union and the United States have voiced their concern. The Israeli authorities, however, have produced figures which show that this simply is not happening – that less than one per cent of new arrivals have chosen life on a West Bank or Gaza Strip settlement. But settlers are bringing groups of Soviet immigrants to visit settlements; and many I spoke to were convinced that in the end, both by individual choice and by a gradual process of seepage, a substantial number of Russian Jews would move into the territories.

The possibility exists still that a peace process will get under way and lead eventually to the surrender of part of the Occupied Territories. There have been predictions that the Jewish-settler population will take up arms and refuse to leave; as mentioned earlier, a group of settlers has drawn up plans to create a 'State of Judea' in the event of an Israeli withdrawal. This group is generally dismissed, though, as representing only a tiny minority of the Jewish inhabitants of the West Bank and Gaza Strip – one settler described the whole idea as a Kahane gimmick. Indeed, my feeling is that if the Israeli government ordered the dismantling of the settlements (and that is a prospect which is hard to imagine) then the overwhelming majority of Jews would leave the Territories after protesting as much as they could. Only a handful would risk a fight with the Israeli army, which would amount to civil war. In April 1982 there were violent scenes in Yamit in the Sinai, when a group of settlers, members of Gush Emunim, tried to defy the government order to leave, but similar resistance in the West Bank would be difficult given that the settlements are so spread out. The authorities could easily cut their supplies of food, water and electricity. Nevertheless, however limited the potential for violence, any Israeli government would think twice before ordering Jews to leave the Territories for fear of the sight of Jewish blood being spilled by fellow Jews.

On the other hand if, as would be more likely, the settlers were given the option to remain, then a large number of men would probably stay to defend their land and property from attacks by the Arabs. 'There would be', as one settler put it, 'a Jewish Intifada.'

The debate about whether or not settlers would stay and fight is hypothetical, but I agree with the view expressed by the settlers themselves that their very presence on the ground lessens the chances of a negotiated settlement being reached with the Palestinians – inside and outside the Occupied Territories. I cannot imagine the international community (with the United States at the forefront) exerting sufficient pressure on a government in Israel to force it either to order the dismantling of the townships or to decree that they should be abandoned. Equally unlikely is the prospect of an Israeli government telling settlers that they are welcome to survive as best they can, without army support, in a state governed by a hostile Palestinian community. Just as the settlements have become rooted to the rocky hilltops of the West Bank, so the attitudes of the Palestinians have become entrenched. If Palestinians were to live in peace and harmony with any Israelis, it's hard to imagine that it would be with the new religious Zionists.

The religious Zionists have constructed townships which in their appearance are Western and which contrast sharply with the plainer styles of the Arab villages. But the Zionists speak with a blind certainty and a blind conviction which are not dissimilar in tone to that of any

Palestinian denouncing the Zionist presence on the land which he calls his own. In other words, both sides are trapped in the strait-jacket of inflexible Middle Eastern attitudes. And just as the forces within the Arab world which might be able to counsel moderation and flexibility find their words falling on deaf ears, so a rightward-leaning and increasingly religion-inspired Israel has little inclination to listen to voices calling for dialogue with the enemy.

What I find worrying is that the inflexibility is becoming institutionalized and accepted by both peoples. It may well be true, for example, that the best known and most-often-quoted settler leaders do not represent the views of the majority of those Jews living in the occupied West Bank and Gaza Strip. But it is alarming that the radical statements and actions of these men are accepted so passively by the Israeli public. Rabbi Moshe Levinger was a founder of Gush Emunim and is one of the most radical and outspoken settlers. In 1979 he led a movement to establish a settler presence in a building which in the 1920s had been Jewish-owned in the centre of Hebron in the occupied West Bank. Never before then or since, in establishing settlements or in protesting against Arab violence, has Rabbi Levinger ducked controversy and publicity. In September 1988 he shot dead a shopkeeper in Hebron after his car was stoned. (The man killed was at the door of his shop at the time and was unconnected with the stoning.) Rabbi Levinger was accused of manslaughter, which carries a maximum sentence of twenty years, but a plea-bargaining deal was struck in the District Court in Jerusalem and the manslaughter charge was dropped. Still, the judge said, the Rabbi had taken the law into his own hands and he added that the punishment should reflect the value of human life. In the end the Rabbi was given a sentence of just five months.

The public outcry was minimal and came from groups on the far left of the political spectrum. But what I found hard to believe was the fact that two days later Rabbi Levinger, having been sentenced to imprisonment for killing a man, was still at liberty. More than that, he was standing next to the speaker of the Knesset and other dignitaries at a religious ceremony in the centre of Nablus. It was an event shrouded in controversy – it involved the presentation of Torah scrolls to Jewish seminary students at Joseph's tomb, which is a site holy both to Jews and Muslims. Because of the controversy and because of fears that the incident might provoke Palestinian anger (since the Palestinians believed the ceremony was designed to mask the creation of a Jewish settlement in the city) the

70,000 strong population of Nablus was put under curfew. Peace Now was allowed to hold a protest at the ceremony, but the nation as a whole seemed to accept without question both Rabbi Levinger's participation in the ceremony in the company of a government official, and the collective punishment of 70,000 Palestinians in order that the ceremony could go ahead.

The Middle East conflict is stuck in the mud. The will to overcome prejudice has been swamped by fatalism and fanaticism, which in turn have been nourished by disillusionment. The established, secular-oriented leadership is in trouble from one end of the region to the other, discredited and despised by many of those it seeks to lead. And the subsequent despair has led many more Israelis and Arabs to turn to religion. But the three religions involved, Judaism, Islam and Christianity, sharing many of the same roots, also claim some of the same sites and some of the same lands. And in the Middle East these religions may preach compassion, but they don't practise it, because they are so closely allied with frustrated political ambitions to dominate land and people. The Islamic fundamentalists want an Islamic state throughout the region which would evict Israel from both the Occupied Territories and the area established as the Jewish state in 1948; Jewish fundamentalists cannot entertain any Arab claim to these lands which, they say, were given to the Jewish people by God.

Against this background of absolutism it is no surprise to see both outbreaks of violence and the corrosion of the values which should lead to the condemnation of that violence. A numbness sets in. Violence becomes commonplace and loses its ability to shock. I saw it in Beirut; I began seeing it in Israel and the Occupied Territories. A Palestinian told me how Israeli troops had forced their way into his house late one night, looking for a particular youth. They ordered him to wake his four children. He demurred, saying that they were all just youngsters. The soldiers then forcibly woke the children. 'Fortunately,' the Palestinian went on, 'the kids are used to this sort of thing, so they weren't scared.' What sort of adults will those children become? What sort of adults will the children of the soldiers become?

Some Israelis are well aware of the erosion of moral values within Israel which the continued occupation of the West Bank and Gaza Strip is causing. The Association for Civil Rights in Israel (Acri), in their report for 1990, pointed out that public commitment in the country to civil rights and democracy had been eroded by the persistent violation of human rights in the Occupied Territories since the start of the Intifada. The Chairman of Acri, Binyamin Tsur, commented: 'Because of what is happening in the Territories we are becoming insensitive to human rights issues. A large proportion of the population sees inequality before the law between Jews and Arabs as justified. People look at it as normal.' So it is that the house of a Palestinian suspected (and only suspected) of, say, throwing a petrol bomb will be demolished. So why, an Israeli lawyer involved in human rights issues wondered, was the house of the (Israeli) man who killed seven Palestinians at Rishon Lezion, south of Tel Aviv, in May 1990 not demolished? If one punishment can be justified, why not the other?

According to Eli Nathan, also of Acri, the problem goes even further. 'When we see in public opinion polls that forty to fifty per cent of the people say there is too much democracy and freedom of the press, and that Arabs should be "transferred" [expelled], it creates a very difficult basis for protecting human rights in Israel. Human rights violated in Nablus [in the West Bank] will ultimately be violated in Tel Aviv and Haifa.' Surveys conducted during the first half of 1990 indicated that more than half of all young Israelis supported the idea that the Arab population should be 'transferred'.

In May 1990, the cry of 'Death to the Arabs' was heard once again on the streets of Jerusalem, in the aftermath of an explosion in the crowded Mahane Yehuda market area of the city which killed one man and wounded several others. Not only were Arabs in the neighbourhood jostled and insulted, but the same treatment was meted out to several cameramen there as well. 'Die, you dirty sons of bitches,' one bearded man wearing a black kippa was heard to shout. The bomb was simply the latest incident in a cycle of violence – action, revenge, reaction – which had begun with the killing earlier in the month of seven Palestinians from the Gaza Strip by a lone Israeli wearing military uniform. Many more Palestinians were killed and wounded in the subsequent days as the Israeli army opened fire to quell riots in the Gaza Strip and elsewhere. And before the end of the month a Palestinian group had tried to launch a seaborne attack on the beaches of Israel using six speedboats. Only one boat reached the shore; four of the Palestinians on board were killed, the rest were captured. The shoot-out happened on a popular beach south of Tel Aviv on a busy holiday. Rumours spread in the area that some of the Palestinians were still at large, and many Israeli civilians, caught in big traffic jams because the roads were sealed off, were seen wielding pistols and automatic rifles as they joined in the hunt for the non-existent Palestinians. The Commissioner of Police later condemned what he called 'this Wild West behaviour'. Again, my thoughts returned to Lebanon, where Wild West behaviour has been normal for many years.

The acts of violence in May 1990 were condemned variously by different people as they happened – I do not claim that there is a total numbness in Israel, or anywhere else in the region. But what was unmistakable was a sense of resignation and helplessness. These sort of acts, it seemed to be acknowledged with an air of fatalism, are inevitable, given the lack of progress towards resolving the whole Middle East problem.

Therefore, for the young Israeli, as much as for the young Syrian or Jordanian, frequent calls to put on military uniform will be part of life for the foreseeable future. The jet fighters will continue to scream across the skies, sonic booms will shake the buildings and everyone will carry on pretending that life is normal. But it is a shallow pretence. The Municipality in Jerusalem sent householders a pamphlet advising them how to prepare and stock bomb shelters. ('Dear Resident, We are turning to you personally, and to the members of your household, to do all you can in order to prepare the city to stand against an enemy attack, which is possible in a time of war. The residents of Jerusalem have learned from experience. Jerusalem has already been the target of enemy attacks twice ...'). With talk of Arab countries acquiring long-range missiles and even nuclear weapons, politicians on the right find a ready audience when they speak, as one did, of 'the waves of danger smashing at Israel from all directions'.

So, the vicious circle continues. As the threats are issued by the Arab nations, so the fortress settlements on the hilltops of the West Bank will be expanded and the fortress mentality of the Israeli people will be strengthened. And if the first step towards Middle East peace involves solving the problem of the Occupied Territories, then peace must be a distant prospect.

For a liberal, secular Israeli who believed in the ideals of the early pioneers, these are depressing days. Old-timers have watched as their values have been eroded and their leaders have been ensnared by a political system which so often puts personal ambition above the interests of either party or state. The long period between governments in 1990 saw public disillusionment and cynicism sink to new depths. President Chaim Herzog spoke of 'unprecedented political and public confusion' and the 'frustration and anger of the electorate'. In the course of conducting street interviews with Israelis during this long hiatus I asked one elderly man for his opinion of the political system. He paused before answering, and then spoke in a voice which was heavy with sadness: 'What shall I say? Miserable. Miserable. I would have expected that Israelis would behave differently. We have lost all belief in politicians. I am very fed up and very disappointed. My disappointment – it hurts terribly.' And so saying, he pulled up the sleeve of his jacket to reveal a number tattooed on his arm. This survivor of the Nazi concentration camps was feeling the disappointment more acutely than many younger Israelis.

Disillusionment contributes, no doubt, to the prickly and rude exterior which so many Israelis show to each other and to outsiders alike. My neighbour told me of an occasion on a bus in Jerusalem when a man boarded and indicated to the driver that he had a bus-pass. 'Just a second,' the driver said, 'I didn't see it properly.' So the man flashed the card in front of the driver a second time. 'I still didn't see your name on it.' The man exploded: 'What kind of bloody country is this where you have to show everyone your ticket, where nobody trusts you?' At this point a woman sitting near the front of the bus piped up. 'It's not the country which is awful, it's the people.' That was the spark which ignited a free-for-all among the rest of the passengers. 'Where else in the world', my neighbour commented, 'would you get on a bus and find that kind of scene?'

Where else would you find a small country with so many people from different backgrounds expressing such a variety of views? It's a melting-pot that seems, at times, on the point of boiling over. Yossi Ben Shon is a television engineer, in his late twenties and born in Israel of Iranian and Turkish parents. 'Our biggest threat is ourselves. All the people here are Jews – you know it's a problem.' He laughed at my expression of amazement and added: 'I'm not joking.'

Every Israeli I know says he wants peace. Peace with the Arabs; security at home. 'Leaving aside the bureaucracy,' Yossi Ben Shon says, 'you can see very clearly in the people how everyone is stressed. Everybody is jumpy. When I go to other countries I feel people are transmitting, you know, calm. Here you have heavy taxes and army duty two months each year. You can feel the country getting to you. You cannot run away from reality here, it's hard.'

Apart from the pressure of external threats and that of daily life, Israel also has to cope with increasing polarization – between left and right, between religious and secular citizens, between Arabs and Jews. Given the divisions within society, it is clear that one advantage of the fortress mentality is the way that it unites Israelis under the national flag in the face of external threat. If that threat were to disappear I believe that the polarization would be even more marked. And I cannot imagine what cohesive force would emerge to hold Israeli society together.

Israel – the state for the Jewish people – is, by definition, unique in a region dominated by Arabs and Islam. It is also a nation of immense inner complexity. But when you look closely and you lay aside preconceptions, you notice that the climate in Israel is not so different from that in the surrounding Arab states. And the outlook for them all is anything but settled.

Nothing could point up the uncertainties of the region more than the crisis in the Gulf which erupted in August 1990 after the Iraqi invasion of Kuwait. In the course of this crisis, which saw a radical shake-up of alliances in the region, President Saddam Hussein of Iraq repeated the threats against Israel which he had made earlier in the year. He also exploited the current resurgence of interest in Islam to win popular Arab support by calling for a Jihad (holy war) against the West and its allies. All these developments strengthened the arguments of those in Israel who advocate the building of new battlements in preparation for possible new battles.

INDEX